Nevada

Nevada

R. Conrad Stein

Children's Press®
A Division of Grolier Publishing
New York   London   Hong Kong   Sydney
Danbury, Connecticut

Frontispiece: Highway 95, Humboldt County

Front cover: Valley of Fire State Park, Overton

Back cover: Old Lincoln County Court House

Consultant: Sue Kendall, Nevada State Library and Archives

Please note: All statistics are as up-to-date as possible at the time of publication.

Visit Children's Press on the Internet at http://publishing.grolier.com

Book production by Editorial Directions, Inc.

Library of Congress Cataloging-in-Publication Data

Stein, R. Conrad.
　　Nevada / R. Conrad Stein.
　　　　144 p. 24 cm. — (America the beautiful. Second series)
　　Includes bibliographical references (p.) and index.
　　Summary : Describes the geography, plants, animals, history, economy, religions,
　　　culture, sports, arts, and people of Nevada.
　　ISBN 0-516-21041-6
　　1. Nevada Juvenile literature. [1. Nevada.] I. Title. II. Series.
F841.3.S74 2000
979.8—dc21

99-28016
CIP

GROLIER
PUBLISHING

©2000 by Children's Press®, a division of Grolier Publishing Co., Inc.
All rights reserved. Published simultaneously in Canada
Printed in the United States of America
1 2 3 4 5 6 7 8 9 10 R 09 08 07 06 05 04 03 02 01 00

Acknowledgments

The author wishes to thank the Nevada Commission on Tourism in
Carson City for its assistance in preparing this book.

Great Basin National Park

Las Vegas

Cathedral Gorge State Park

Contents

Desert tortoise

Fishing at Lake Tahoe

Carson City

Virginia City steam train

Reno Balloon Race

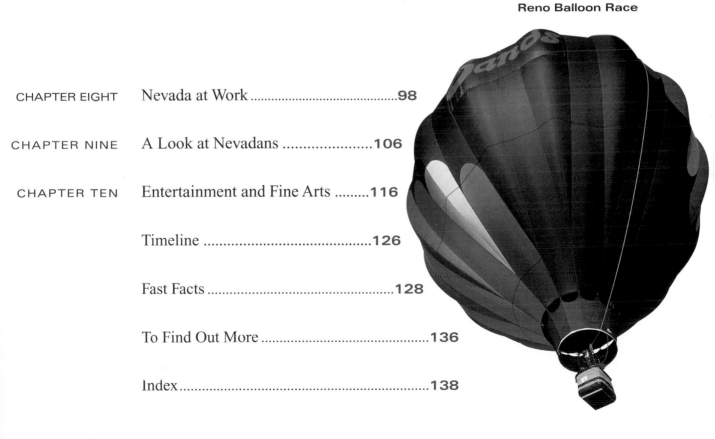

CHAPTER ONE

The Silver State

Very little comes easy in Nevada. Yes, at one time miners found gold and silver ore under the soil, and some grew rich almost overnight. But the mineral strike was an exception in Nevada's history. For the most part, the state's land is stingy. Less rain falls on Nevada than on any of the forty-nine other states. Most of its land area is desert. When the nation began its great push westward in the 1850s and 1860s, settlers hastened to get *through* Nevada quickly on their way to more inviting places such as California and Oregon.

In the last quarter of the twentieth century, however, Nevada became the fastest-growing state. The population increased 51 percent in the 1980s alone. A huge tourist industry provides employment and attracts new residents. Every year almost

Much of Nevada is considered to be desert.

Opposite: Fishing at Cave Lake

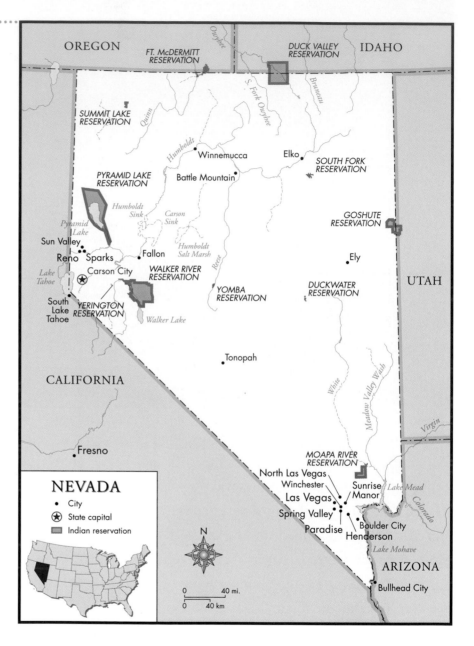

OREGON
FT. McDERMITT
RESERVATION
DUCK VALLEY
RESERVATION
IDAHO

Ouyhee

S. Fork Ouyhee

Bruneau

SUMMIT LAKE
RESERVATION

Quinn

Humboldt

• Winnemucca
Elko •
SOUTH FORK
RESERVATION

PYRAMID LAKE
RESERVATION
Battle Mountain •

GOSHUTE
RESERVATION

*Humboldt
Sink*
*Carson
Sink*

*Pyramid
Lake*

Sun Valley •
*Humboldt
Salt Marsh*
Ely •

Reno • Sparks
• Fallon
Reese

Carson City •
WALKER RIVER
RESERVATION

DUCKWATER
RESERVATION

*Lake
Tahoe*

South
Lake
Tahoe
YERINGTON
RESERVATION
YOMBA
RESERVATION

Walker Lake

• Tonopah

CALIFORNIA

White

Meadow Valley Wash

Virgin

• Fresno

MOAPA RIVER
RESERVATION

North Las Vegas •
Winchester •
Sunrise *Lake Mead*

NEVADA
• City
⭐ State capital
▨ Indian reservation
Las Vegas • Manor
Spring Valley •
Paradise •
Boulder City
Henderson •

Colorado

N

Lake Mohave

ARIZONA
Bullhead City •

0   40 mi.
0   40 km

UTAH

**Geopolitical map
of Nevada**

40 million out-of-state visitors come to Nevada and about
35 percent of Nevada's workers hold tourist-related jobs.

Many critics contend that tourists flock to Nevada for wrong or
even immoral reasons. The state is home to gambling casinos where

about $7.7 billion is passed over tables each year. Nevada is also famous—or infamous—for quick marriages, divorces, and adult entertainment. Its largest town, Las Vegas, is sometimes called Sin City.

Yet those who denounce Nevada for the vices it offers fail to look at the whole picture. Nevada is a spectacularly beautiful state. In addition to

The Sierra Nevada mountains are part of the state's beautiful landscape.

its sprawling deserts, it has crystal-clear streams and sparkling lakes. An evergreen forest in the Sierra Nevada—translated literally as "snow-covered mountain range"—is a delight to skiers and hikers. Even the gambling casinos have labored to change their reputations. In the 1990s, Las Vegas spent millions of dollars on family-oriented hotels.

Inventiveness is the theme of the Nevada story. The land was too dry for large-scale farming, and the population was too small to carry out massive industrial projects. So Nevadans turned to tourism to make a living on their beautiful if somewhat parched land. The effort has reaped rewards. For the past decade, Nevada has enjoyed low unemployment and a growing economy.

Nevada is a western state, and its past is a chapter in the exciting history of the American West. Silver mining gave rise to one of its nicknames—the Silver State—and stories of the Old West are Nevada's pride. The people regard their history as an adventure.

CHAPTER TWO

Nevada's Distant Past

About 20,000 years ago, bands of people living in Asia began an amazing migration. In small groups they crossed land and ice bridges and entered the American continent. Before this migration, there were no humans in the Americas. Those early travelers, ancestors of the American Indians, were hunters. They probably followed shifting herds of animals onto the American continent. Some experts claim the Asian people arrived in the Americas 40,000 years ago.

Early inhabitants of Nevada often lived in caves.

Ancient Nevada

What did the long-ago travelers find when they entered Nevada? First, the land they discovered was much wetter than the present-day state. At that time, the world was recovering from the long Ice Age. Melting ice created rivers and lakes, breeding a fantastic variety of plants and animals. Nevada was the home of exotic beasts, such as mammoths, mastodons, and giant sloths. The bones of mastodons have been found at Walker Lake near the city of Hawthorne. Spear points embodied in those bones indicate that

Opposite: Petroglyphs at Grimes Point

Spirit Cave Man

In 1940, the well-preserved body of an ancient man was found at Spirit Cave, not far from Salt Wells in Churchill County. It seemed the body was placed in the cave as part of a funeral service. The man was carefully wrapped in mats made of woven reeds. He wore a robe of animal skin and had animal skin moccasins on his feet. In 1994, Spirit Cave Man was tested using advanced radiocarbon methods. Experts determined the body was laid to rest some 9,500 years ago.

Spirit Cave Man was 5 feet 2 inches (1.6 m) tall and probably forty years old. A crack in his cranium indicates he suffered a fractured skull, which might have been the cause of his death. He also had badly rotted teeth. Spirit Cave Man lived in an age when tools were crude, but the reed mats covering his body were woven into precise diamond-shaped patterns that exhibit marvelous skill. The remains of Spirit Cave Man are now at the Nevada State Museum in Carson City. ■

A Clovis point spearhead

this region was a hunting ground for ancient people.

The first Nevadans lived in caves or in rock shelters. A cave at Winnemucca Lake contains human bones believed to be 11,000 years old. The people of this era survived by fishing, hunting, and gathering wild fruits and berries. They hunted with spears and small stone darts.

The development of the stone Clovis point spearhead brought a revolution among the early Indians. This type of spearhead was named after the spot in New

Mexico where it was first discovered. Clovis point spearheads, about 5 inches (13 centimeters) long, were skillfully carved and tapered at the base to allow them to fit firmly on a pole. These very effective spear points allowed hunters to kill large animals, and wandering bands may have taught one another how to make them. Clovis point spearheads have been discovered near the Nevada towns of Beatty and Tonopah.

About 6,000 years ago, men and women lived in the vicinity of Lovelock, in the northwestern part of the state. Stone tools

Petroglyphs

Near the town of Fallon lie marshlands that were inhabited continuously for more than 6,000 years. Over the centuries, the people living there carved symbolic pictures called petroglyphs on the rocks. At Grimes Point, you can see these curious scratches on the face of cliffs. Some look like snakes or stick figures. Others look strangely like tic-tac-toe games. ■

and other tokens of their culture have been unearthed at Lovelock Cave and at the nearby Leonard Rock Shelter. The rock
shelter has curious drawings that may represent animals. Indians at Lovelock Cave also wove dry reeds into very clever duck
decoys. By floating their reed creations in ponds and lakes, the
Lovelock people attracted ducks that they then killed with darts
or stones.

Gradually, life in Nevada began to change. The glacial lakes
dried up, and the roaring rivers dwindled to streams. Huge animals
such as the mammoth and the mastodon died out. The Indians of
Nevada had to learn how to live on a drier, less bountiful land.

The Nevada State Museum

Life in Nevada as it looked 10,000 years ago can be seen at the Nevada State Museum in Carson City. A model of a mammoth is displayed there are valued items of ancient peoples including spear points and a spear-throwing device called an *atlatl*. ■

The Lost City Museum

The largest Anasazi towns in Nevada were built along the Virgin and Muddy River Valleys in the southern part of the state. Many of those towns were submerged when Hoover Dam was built in the 1930s, creating Lake Mead.

A glimpse of Anasazi life can be seen at the Lost City Museum near Overton. The museum, which resembles a grand Anasazi house, holds an extensive display of tools, pottery, and exhibits depicting the life of these long-ago people. ■

Farmers and Wanderers

An ingenious people called the Anasazi built the first complex farming civilization in what is now the American West. Their greatest cities were built in Arizona and New Mexico, but their influence spread to Nevada. Beginning about A.D. 700, Anasazi farmers felled trees, plowed ground, and planted corn, beans, and squash. They also dammed rivers to create irrigation for their fields. The word *Anasazi* has several interpretations. It is often translated from the Navajo language as "the ancient ones."

Farming gave the Anasazi time to develop skills in arts and

crafts. They made brightly painted pottery, shards of which have been uncovered in southern Nevada. Their straw baskets were woven so tightly that they could carry water without it leaking. The Anasazi built houses out of rock or mud bricks. Like modern apartment buildings, their dwellings consisted of many rooms covered by one roof. Near Overton are the ruins of an Anasazi building that had ninety-four rooms.

Anasazi culture flourished until about A.D. 1200. Then, for unknown reasons, the civilization died out. Tree rings indicate a killer drought struck the American West at the time of the Anasazi decline and lasted more than twenty years. War might also have contributed to the culture's doom.

New tribes occupied Nevada. The Shoshone lived in the river valleys to the north. The Washo people resided around beautiful Lake Tahoe in the Sierras. The Northern and Southern Paiute became desert dwellers. All were nomadic hunters—wandering peoples who knew little about farming. Without the luxury of steady crops, they never developed the artistic skills practiced by the Anasazi.

Nevada Indian groups of the post-Anasazi period spoke different languages, but they held many beliefs in common. They believed in an all-powerful creator and in a host of lesser gods or spirits. The people of old Nevada found spiritual forces just about everywhere—in rocks, in clumps of sagebrush, even in morning mists or fogs. Animals were thought to be messengers of the gods. The appearance of a wolf was a sign of good fortune, while a lurking coyote meant sickness and bad luck. The mountain people thought that killing a bear gave a hunter courage and strength. It was generally believed that a person rose to a happier realm at death and that the spirits of the dead watched over the living.

The search for food was never-ending for the men and women of old Nevada. Only the Southern Paiute practiced farming, but they farmed at a primitive level. Those living near lakes and rivers caught fish and waterfowl. Pine nuts were a major source of food for tribes near the Sierras. Rabbits were considered a treat for the desert-dwelling Northern Paiute. The Indians of the desert often ate grasshoppers. First, they forced the grasshoppers into a small area as if they were herding cattle. Then they beat the insects with flat sticks, making a paste that gave the Indians a life-sustaining, if not a tasty, meal.

The Paiute were one of the Native American tribes that lived in early Nevada.

Native Americans sometimes lived in structures made of grass and poles.

The Native Americans of Nevada lived in groups of about 100 people. Frequently, these bands got together to hunt or to gather pine nuts. Sometimes the bands fought, but the constant quest for food usually left them too busy or too exhausted to engage in warfare. Only in the winter months did Nevadan Indians settle down and live in one spot. Then they built dwellings of poles covered with grass or reeds, and there was time for play. Small children made toys out of mud. Young men engaged in a sort of soccer game. They also enjoyed gambling games, using small sticks as dice. Music was made with drums, rattles, and flutes carved from animal bones. Dancing was considered to be a way to contact the spirits.

In 1521, Spanish forces conquered Mexico, far to the south. About 100 years later, the English established settlements on the Atlantic Coast. Eventually these societies would affect Nevada.

Explorers from Afar

Seeking new lands, the Spaniards pushed out of Mexico in the late 1500s. Their most successful settlement was Santa Fe, New Mexico, which they established in 1610. From their base in New Mexico, the Spaniards claimed a huge tract of land that included California, Texas, Arizona, Utah, Colorado, and Nevada.

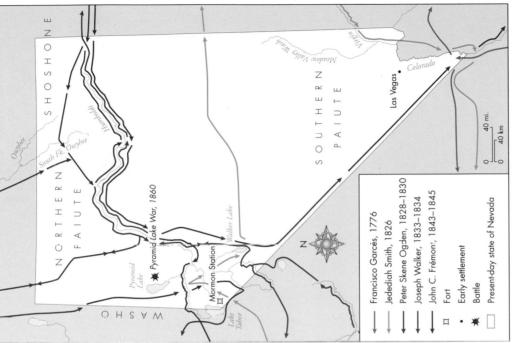

Exploration of Nevada

Map labels:
SHOSHONE

NORTHERN PAIUTE

WASHO

SOUTHERN PAIUTE

Owyhee
South Fk. Owyhee
Humboldt
Pyramid Lake
Pyramid Lake War, 1860
Mormon Station
Lake Tahoe
Walker Lake
Meadow Valley Wash
Virgin
Las Vegas
Colorado

N

0   40 mi.
0   40 km

Francisco Garcés, 1776
Jedediah Smith, 1826
Peter Skene Ogden, 1828–1830
Joseph Walker, 1833–1834
John C. Frémont, 1843–1845
☒ Fort
• Early settlement
✳ Battle
☐ Present-day state of Nevada

The first European to see Nevada was probably Francisco Garcés, a Spanish priest. Garcés journeyed north in 1776 seeking a route from New Mexico to California. Spanish travelers later gave the future state its name when they saw the rugged mountains to the west and called them the *Nevadas*, Spanish for "snow covered." Nevada, however, was Spanish by claim only. No large groups of Spaniards ever settled there.

People in the United States looked upon the West as a territory that was destined to be theirs. Americans even coined the term *Manifest Destiny*, which meant it was God's will for their nation to extend from the Atlantic Ocean to the Pacific.

The first U.S. explorers to enter Nevada were fur trappers. In the East, beaver and fox pelts were crafted into fancy hats, making the animal skins almost as valuable as gold. The fur trapper Jedediah Smith entered Nevada in 1826 and discovered only deserts. "We frequently traveled without water sometimes for two days over sandy deserts, where there was no sign of vegetation," Smith wrote. Completing his gloomy report, Smith called Nevada, "completely barren and destitute." Smith and his men were forced

Joseph Walker, a mountain man

John C. Frémont's expedition to Pyramid Lake

to eat their own horses to survive. Peter Skene Ogden (for whom the city of Ogden, Utah, is named) led a group of fur trappers to Nevada in 1828. Ogden discovered a broad river, which was later called the Humboldt, after the great German geographer Alexander von Humboldt.

Joseph Walker was a mountain man, one of a famous group of adventurers who lived lonely and dangerous lives in the wilds of the West. Mountain men trapped fur-bearing animals and explored unknown lands in the process. In 1833, Walker led a band of about fifty men into Nevada and fought the first battle between Indians and whites on Nevada soil. The Indians, who had never seen firearms before, lost about forty warriors.

John C. Frémont was an officer in the U.S. Army. In the 1840s, Frémont trekked over Nevada making maps and blazing trails. He discovered the Carson River, naming it for his guide, the famous mountain man Kit Carson. Frémont found a sparkling lake near the Sierras and called it Pyramid Lake because of its giant pyramid-shaped rock formation. He also noted that the rivers in this region do not flow into the sea. Instead the rivers either dry up or empty into inland lakes. Therefore he called the land the Great Basin, a name it has to this day.

In 1821, Mexican patriots overthrew Spanish rule and established the nation of Mexico. This meant that Mexico now claimed the western lands, which included Nevada. Between 1846 and 1848, Mexico

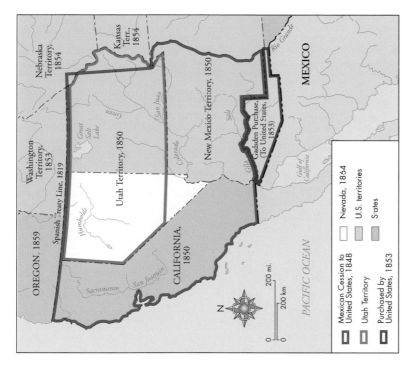

Historical map of Nevada

and the United States fought a bitter war that proved a disaster for Mexico. The United States gained what became Texas, Arizona, western New Mexico, California, Utah, western Colorado, and Nevada. For Nevada, the change of ownership meant little because there was not a single settler, American or Mexican, living there at the time. Still, Manifest Destiny was now a reality—the United States stretched from sea to sea. And Nevada was firmly a part of this dynamic nation.

Chapter Three

Pioneering in the Silver State

n 1848, a foreman who worked for John Sutter noticed a strange sparkle in a California stream. He reached into the water and picked up a pebble about the size of a kernel of corn. That tiny speck was pure gold, and it brought a human stampede to California. In 1849 alone, some 85,000 prospectors swarmed into the once sleepy region. The great California Gold Rush changed the American West forever.

Travelers and Settlers

They came on foot, they came on horseback, and they rode in wagons. All were prospectors hurrying to the California goldfields, choking on the dust of the Nevada deserts and cursing the infernal land. One gold seeker wrote to others planning to make the trip,

Opposite: Stagecoaches in the Sierra Nevada in 1865

"[In Nevada] expect to find the worst desert you ever saw, and then find it worse than you expected."

It took roughly six months for Gold Rush prospectors to hike from the eastern states to California. The most-feared tract of land in their journey was a parched area in the heart of Nevada called the Forty-Mile Desert. There, with every step, the prospectors sank up to their ankles in dust. The trail along the Forty-Mile Desert became littered with dead animals and broken-down wagons. Crosses and crude gravestones also marked the trail.

For California emigrants, Nevada was more a path—and not a very pleasant path—than it was a place. Yet some forward-looking people saw promise in Nevada.

One such visionary was Brigham Young, the forceful leader of the Mormon Church. The Mormons had been expelled from Illi-

The Ill-fated Donner Party

In 1846, a group of eighty-seven settlers bound for California made their way from Illinois along the Humboldt River. The group hoped to establish farms in the new land. Well supplied with dozens of ox-drawn wagons, the party was led by brothers George and Jacob Donner. Trouble began as they crossed the Nevada desert and trekked under the scorching sun without water for three days. Cattle went mad and stampeded. People saw fantastic visions of lakes and

waterfalls, and at least one man went insane.

At the base of the Sierra Nevada, the Donner party took what they believed to be a shortcut to California. It was a disastrous decision. An early snowfall closed the pass through the mountains and stranded the people. Of the original members of the Donner party, only forty-seven survived. To live through that terrible winter, they ate shoe leather. Some ate the flesh of their dead comrades. ∎

nois because neighboring communities objected to their polygamy (the practice of having more than one wife at a time). Seeking freedom to practice their religion, the Mormons marched into the western wilderness and reached what is now Salt Lake City, Utah, in 1847. According to legend, Brigham Young took one look at the Great Salt Lake and said simply, "This is the place." He and his followers then set to work building a city. From their base at Salt Lake, the Mormons sent pioneers to nearby areas, including Nevada.

In 1851, the Mormons established a fort at the Sierra Nevada just south of present-day Reno. That log fort was the first substantial structure built in Nevada since Anasazi times. Residents of Mormon Station, the community that developed around the fort, traded goods with California-bound travelers. Mormon Station was later renamed Genoa, and today it is considered to be Nevada's first non-Indian town.

Through most of the 1850s, Nevada was part of the huge Utah Territory. Brigham Young served as Utah Territory's first governor. Gradually Mormon and non-Mormon families arrived and set up farms in the Carson River Valley not far from Genoa. A sawmill was built at a new village named Franktown. In 1855, the Mormons established another trading post at a spring and meadowland called Las Vegas. The Mormons abandoned Las Vegas, but eventually it became Nevada's largest city.

Although the settlers in Carson Valley were few in number, they had problems. Non-Mormons resented being governed by Mormon leaders. At one point, the non-Mormons of the Carson Valley asked Congress to unite their community with California. Then, in 1857, Brigham Young had a disagreement with the federal gov-

Heroic Mailman

The early settlers of the Carson Valley got their mail from Sacramento, California, so mail carriers had to journey on foot through the Sierra Nevada carrying the mail in backpacks. They made this tough five-day hike even in the dead of winter and thus became heroes to the letter-hungry pioneers. The greatest of all mail carriers was a Norwegian immigrant known as "Snowshoe" Thompson (left). He fashioned two planks out of tree bark into what served as both snowshoes and skis. The planks were about 10 feet (3 m) long. With them, Thompson sailed through the mountain passes faster than any other mail carrier. ■

ernment. Fearing an invasion by the U.S. Army, Young recalled all Mormons to Salt Lake City. After the recall, Mormon influence faded in the western regions of Utah Territory.

The Comstock Bonanza

During the 1850s, only a few California-bound prospectors stopped to see if there was gold in the hills of Nevada. Several of them struck pay dirt by finding nuggets and gold dust. The scant amount of gold they discovered, however, could not compare to the excitement that California offered. There, stories said, lucky miners became millionaires overnight.

James Finney was one of several prospectors who roamed Nevada's Washoe Mountains seeking gold. James Finney was nicknamed "Old Virginny," after his home state of Virginia. He had been a prospector for years with almost no success. It was rumored he lived in Utah Territory because he was on the run from the law in California. In 1859, Finney dug into what looked like a promising hill and chanced upon the Comstock Lode. It proved to be the richest deposit of silver ore ever found in the United States.

Miners working the Comstock Lode

Experienced miners on the scene were puzzled by the black stuff that was mixed in with Comstock gold. The Nevada miners had little experience with silver. It is said that a miner from Mexico looked at the black substance, grew excited, and told the others that it was valuable silver ore. However, no one spoke Spanish, so they were unable to understand the exuberant Mexican. They soon learned, however, that the Nevada hills contained fabulous amounts of silver. Gold was also found in the Comstock Lode, but actually it was a silver bonanza.

The silver strike triggered a rush in reverse. From California, thousands of prospectors descended on Nevada, the place they had cursed just a few years earlier. Suddenly, Nevada was a paradise where a hardworking prospector could earn $1,000 a day.

Why Was It Called the Comstock Lode?

Fellow miners said Henry Comstock (right) spent too much time alone in the hills. He talked to himself and made up wild stories about the vast deposits of gold that he had discovered. Around mining camps, he was generally dismissed as a madman. Comstock insisted he owned the land where James "Old Virginny" Finney found the gold. Few took his claims seriously, and Henry Comstock soon vanished from Nevada's mining picture. But he boasted of his ownership claims in a loud and vigorous manner, and history recorded the Nevada ore strike as the Comstock Lode. ■

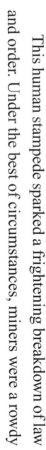

Changing shifts at a Nevada silver mine

Silver mining was dangerous and grueling work. Prospectors chipped away at mountains to create shafts and extract ore. In human-made caves they worked in the dark, sometimes in water up to their knees, and they always feared a cave-in would bury them under tons of soil. But the possible payoff was worth the risks, and miners swarmed to Nevada.

The writer J. Ross Browne lived in Nevada when the Comstock boom began. He left us this description of the great influx of miners streaming into the region: "An almost continuous string of [prospectors and their wagons] stretched like a great snake dragging its slow length as far as the eye could see. In the course of a day's tramp we passed parties of every description and color: Irishmen, wheeling their blankets, provisions, and mining implements on wheelbarrows; American, French, and German foot-passengers, leading heavily laden horses, or carrying their packs on their backs; . . . Mexicans, driving long trains of pack mules; . . . dapper-looking gentlemen, apparently from San Francisco, mounted on fancy horses; women, in men's clothes, mounted on mules or burros; whisky peddlers, organ grinders, drovers, white-haired old men, cripples and hunchbacks, even sick men from their beds—all stark mad for silver."

This human stampede sparked a frightening breakdown of law and order. Under the best of circumstances, miners were a rowdy

William Stewart, Comstock Lawyer

Sometimes Comstock miners with disputed claims battled each other in court rather than on the streets. Lawyer William Stewart (1827–1909) from New York was famous in the Comstock for his keen mind and tough tactics in court. Stewart was a giant man with a flowing yellow beard. He once grew annoyed when another lawyer, half his size, repeatedly inter-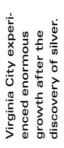rupted him in court. He growled at the man, "You little shrimp, if you interrupt me again I'll eat you alive." The opposing lawyer said, "If you do that you'll have more brains in your belly than in your head." After that exchange, the two became friends. Stewart later had a long political career, serving several terms as Nevada's U.S. senator. ■

bunch, quick to get into fights. Now the greed generated by the silver strike led to horrific violence and bloodshed. Gun battles between rival miners were common events. Hoodlums came to mining camps as much to kill and rampage as to seek silver and gold. One such troublemaker was "Fightin'" Sam Brown, who was rumored to have killed a dozen men in knife fights and gun duels.

One day, Brown picked on a Dutch farmer who shot him dead. A jury freed the farmer, saying "Brown came to his end by the dispensation of a Divine Providence."

Lying in the midst of the Comstock Lode was Virginia City, which grew from a tent camp to a town of 15,000 people in just two years. Legend says that a drunken prospector

Virginia City experienced enormous growth after the discovery of silver.

Mark Twain in Virginia City in 1864

named the city after his home state, Virginia, and then baptized it by breaking a bottle of whiskey on a rock. The town soon had scores of hastily built wooden houses, three theaters, four churches, forty-two saloons, and a newspaper called the *Territorial Enterprise.* Working for that newspaper was a young reporter named Samuel Clemens, who later used the pen name Mark Twain. Of a typical night in Virginia City, Twain wrote, "I have just heard five pistol shots down the street— as such things are in my line I will go and see about it. . . . The pistol did its work well . . . [and] shot two [men] through the heart— both died."

The sudden invasion of miners, prospectors, and other settlers stirred the anger of Nevada's Native Americans. The whites killed game animals on American Indian hunting grounds. They chopped down trees to use as supports for their silver mines, thus depriving the Indians of their staple food, pine nuts.

In early 1860, a band of Paiute Indians killed three white men and burned a cabin. The Indians claimed that the whites had kidnapped three Indian women. News of the murders raced from camp to camp. An army of 105 white men was quickly assembled and marched out. On May 12, the Paiute led this untrained army

Numaga, Man of Peace

Before the Pyramid Lake War began, one man begged his people to keep the peace. He was Numaga, a young Paiute chief. A historian later interviewed the Paiute and recorded the speech Numaga gave to tribal leaders just days before the fighting broke out:

"You would make war on the whites? I ask you to pause and reflect. The white men are like the stars over your heads. You have [suffered] wrongs, great wrongs. . . . But can you, from the mountaintops, reach out and blot out those stars?"

into a carefully prepared trap at a ravine near Pyramid Lake. In a brutally effective ambush, the Indians killed seventy-six whites. The survivors straggled back to the Comstock settlements to tell bloodcurdling stories of the massacre.

The first battle of what was called the Pyramid Lake War spread panic among the whites. Settlers boarded up cabins and gathered together in makeshift forts. The people of Silver City attempted to make a wooden cannon. A force of 550 volunteers was assembled in the Comstock region. The men met where the town of Wadsworth now stands and moved grimly toward the Paiute camp. In a brief and gory clash, some 160 Indians were killed, with little loss of life among the whites. The Pyramid Lake War was the last major conflict with Indians in Nevada.

Statehood, Progress, and Depression

By 1861, the Comstock mining camps held about 7,000 people, and Nevada became a territory separate from Utah Territory. President Abraham Lincoln appointed James W. Nye, a New York

James W. Nye was appointed territorial governor by President Lincoln in 1861.

politician, as territorial governor. Lincoln, however, had more to worry about than the far-flung Nevada Territory. By the time Lincoln took office in March 1861, seven Southern states had seceded, or broken away, from the United States. In April, the bloody Civil War began.

Slavery was the root cause of the Civil War. On the surface, slavery was hardly an issue in Nevada Territory. Technically there were no slaves there, and only about fifty African-Americans lived among the settlers. Still, Lincoln looked with interest upon Nevada. If Nevada became a state, it would automatically send two senators and one representative to Washington, D.C., and Lincoln reasoned that those politicians would be pro-North and friendly to his government. Also, Lincoln needed Nevada's silver to pay the war's enormous expenses.

Although most of Nevada's residents favored the Union and opposed slavery, they certainly did not speak with one voice. Many prospectors who rushed into the Comstock region were Southerners and retained their old loyalties. In typical miner fashion, arguments over Civil War issues accelerated into fistfights and worse. At one point, Southern sympathizers armed with guns tried to take over Virginia City.

The law required a territory to have a population of 127,381 before it qualified for statehood, and Nevada's population did not

The Gridley Sack of Flour

Reuel Gridley (right) owned a grocery store in the town of Austin. A Southern sympathizer, Gridley lost a bet and was forced to parade down Austin's main street carrying a 50-pound (23-kg) sack of flour. The winner of the bet wrote pro-Union messages on the sack. Gridley later became a convert to the Union. He auctioned the sack and sent the proceeds to Northern charities. In all, he raised more than $260,000 in gold and silver for the North. Gridley's charity work consumed so much time, however, that his grocery store went bankrupt. ■

even approach that figure. Nevertheless, Lincoln hurried the statehood process along. Nevada became the thirty-sixth state on October 31, 1864. Carson City was declared its capital. Nevada was the only state to enter the Union during the Civil War years (1861–1865), and therefore it has been called the Battle Born State ever since.

The end of the Civil War saw Nevada's silver mines producing ore worth $23 million a year. Towns such as Lovelock, Unionville, Minden, and Dayton developed. A second silver strike in eastern Nevada led to the rise of Panaca, Pioche, and Eureka. The state's early population was made up largely of men. Women arrived later and helped to civilize Nevada. Soon, churches were built, and when Nevada became a state, it had eight schoolhouses.

The pioneers in Nevada as well as in other regions in the western United States suffered loneliness and isolation from the rest of the country. Letters from eastern states took three to six months to reach Nevada settlements. Children were born, marriages were celebrated, and family members died without the knowledge of relatives in the faraway West.

John Mackay, Silver King

John Mackay (1831–1902) was one of many miners who went to California hoping to find gold and then recrossed the mountains to Nevada to search for silver. In 1872, the Irish-born Mackay struck what was called the Big Bonanza at Virginia City. In five years, his mine yielded $150 million in silver. The Silver King used his money to benefit the state by building churches and contributing to charitable causes. After his death, Mackay's son donated $2 million to establish the Mackay School of Mines in memory of his father at the University of Nevada in Reno. ◼

Westerners hailed the Pony Express, which began service in April 1860. Atop swift horses, the "pony riders" raced with the mail from St. Joseph, Missouri, to Sacramento, California—a distance of almost 2,000 miles (3,218 kilometers)—in an amazing ten days. The Pony Express route ran through Nevada and had a major station at Carson City. Writer Mark Twain gave this stirring description of a young hero delivering the mail at full gallop: "HERE HE COMES! Away across the endless dead level of the prairie a black speck appears against the sky. . . . In a second or two it becomes a horse and rider, rising and falling, rising and falling—sweeping towards us . . . another instant a whoop and a hurrah . . . and a man and horse burst past our excited faces, and go winging away like a belated fragment of a storm!"

The West was truly united with the rest of the country when the transcontinental railroad was completed in 1869. Now a single track stretched from the Mississippi River to San Francisco. Trains carried passengers, goods, and mail. Most important, that iron band marked the completion of Manifest Destiny. Pioneers in

Nevada remembered when it took six months to travel from the eastern states to the West. The same trip could now be made in little more than six days.

Railroads brought settlers from around the world into Nevada. By the 1870s, almost half the population of Nevada was foreign-born. French Canadians worked as lumberjacks in Sierra Nevada forests, Germans established farms in the Carson Valley, Irish toiled in mines of the Comstock Lode, Chinese built railroads and founded small businesses, while Basques from Spain tended sheep, and Italians worked on ranches.

The **Central Pacific Railroad passing through Nevada in 1869**

Ghost Towns

Nevada's boom-and-bust economy produced ghost towns—communities that thrived for twenty or thirty years, but were abandoned when the boom times ended. By some estimates, modern Nevada has 600 ghost towns or "almost" ghost towns. It is a haunting experience to walk down a ghost town's main street today and imagine how it looked when it was packed with laughing and shouting people.

Mining silver was literally "making money," as the government used silver in most of its coins. Nevada, the nation's primary supplier of silver, enjoyed its boom years. Then two developments ended the high times. First, Nevada's richest silver ore was mined

Belmont in Nye County is listed as an "almost" ghost town because it now has about a dozen full-time residents. In the 1860s and 1870s, Belmont was home to more than 2,000 people, and its mines produced $15 million in silver and lead ore. Star performers appeared at its opera house. Today, Belmont's courthouse, the opera house, and dozens of houses stand as charming ghosts of the past. ■

out. Then, in the 1870s, the U.S. government decided to rely on gold more than on silver for its coins. This move reduced the demand for silver. The mines kept producing, but Nevada's silver bonanza was over.

To a certain extent, the decrease in the silver industry brought diversity to Nevada's economy. The state's first resort hotels opened at Lake Tahoe and served tourists. The sheep and cattle business expanded. These measures, however, could not save the state from creeping depression. The population dropped from 62,000 in 1880 to 47,000 in 1890 as workers sought jobs elsewhere.

Silver, gold, lead, and other mining operations never died in Nevada, but clearly the people could no longer rely on these enterprises for a living. Nevadans were reminded that, the mining boom aside, nothing comes easy in their dry and rugged land. If they hoped to see Nevada progress, its people would have to find more inventive ways to make their living.

CHAPTER FOUR

Twentieth-
Century
Nevada

The championship fight between Corbett and Fitzsimmons in March 1897

Opposite: Hoover Dam during construction in 1935

n 1897, noisy crowds descended on Carson City to watch a boxing match between heavyweights Bob Fitzsimmons and "Gentleman Jim" Corbett. At that time, prizefighting was thought of as a lowly activity that appealed only to criminal elements. No matter. Nevada leaders approved of the fight because they were desperate to bring visitors with money into the state. For fourteen bloody rounds, the two boxers battered each other. At ringside, spectators bet feverishly, exchanging thousands of dollars. A crew recorded the match with a new device, a motion-picture camera. The bout was a financial success for the state and set in motion the idea that perhaps tourism and gambling could bring new life to Nevada's struggling economy.

Nevada Grows Up

From Nevada's beginnings as a state, California businessmen ruled the business scene. The owners of the major silver mines lived in California, the banks that financed mine and ranching operations had their main offices in California, and the California-based Central Pacific Railroad set Nevada's freight fees.

In May 1900, this California dominance ended. It happened after a Nevada rancher named James Butler went looking for

Goldfield was a bustling mining town in the early 1900s.

a burro that had strayed. He found the animal in a mountainous area the Indians called the Tonopah. He also stumbled across some rocks that he thought might contain silver ore. Butler chipped some of the rocks loose and gave them to Tasker Oddie, the district attorney of Nye County. The rocks proved to be another silver bonanza. Over the next few years, the Tonopah region yielded from $125 million to $150 million in silver ore. Butler became a millionaire, and Oddie served as Nevada's governor and later as its U.S. senator. Renewed interest in mining led to copper finds at Ruth, Ely, and Mountain City. In 1903, gold was found 25 miles (40 km) south of Tonopah and miners established a village that they appropriately named Goldfield.

Mining operations, however, led to bitter labor strife. Mine owners in Goldfield accused workers of high-grading—the practice of sticking handfuls of rich ore in their pockets and then walking out of the mine with it at the end of their shift. To prevent high-grading, the owners insisted that workers change clothes under the watchful eyes of supervisors before they left the mine. The workers refused, and a strike broke out in 1907. The owners persuaded Nevada governor John Sparks to call in U.S. Army troops because they claimed workers were planning to dynamite the mines. Pas-

Anne Martin, Women's Rights Crusader

Anne Henrietta Martin (1875–1951) was born in Empire City at a time when respectable women were supposed to stay at home and not meddle in politics. Beginning in her teen years, Martin broke from this tradition. She led the Nevada movement to secure voting rights for women. She was a pacifist, opposing America's entry into World War I. In 1918, she ran for the U.S. Senate—the first woman to seek that office in any state. Martin was also a history professor at the University of Nevada and a state tennis champion. ■

sions finally dwindled, but the strike at Goldfield stands as the worst labor conflict in Nevada history.

In 1917, the United States entered World War I (1914–1918). Almost 1,500 volunteer soldiers from Nevada joined the ranks. Prices for copper and other minerals rose. Increased demand also brought prosperity to the state's farms and its cattle and sheep ranches. Farming enjoyed a major boost when Nevada's Newlands Irrigation Project was completed in 1907. The project created dams in the Truckee and Carson Rivers and transformed nonproductive land around the town of Fallon into a fertile agricultural region.

The 1920s were a decade of prosperity for the United States, but Nevada enjoyed only a small share of the national good times. In 1919, after World War I ended, prices for the state's minerals and produce from its farms and ranches dropped. The 1930s brought the Great Depression to the United States. Across the nation, one out of every four workers lost his or her job, and the unemployment rate was even higher in Nevada.

Nevada's joblessness was reduced by a massive effort to build Hoover Dam (originally called Boulder Dam) along the Arizona-

Key Pittman, the Silver Senator

Key Pittman (1877–1940), the senator from Nevada, argued endlessly to retain silver as the national currency. Pittman served twenty-eight years in the U.S. Senate and was clearly the state's most influential man in Washington, D.C. His pro-silver speeches were so fiery that he became known as the Silver Senator. ■

Hoover Dam had a major effect on Nevada and all of the American West.

Nevada border. Some 5,000 men and women worked five years to complete the task. Newspapers hailed Hoover Dam as the largest construction project since the ancient Egyptians built the pyramids. The wall of the great dam was higher than a sixty-story building and so thick it could accommodate a two-lane highway on its top. More than 7 million tons of concrete were poured into the dam, enough to build a 16-foot (5-meter)-wide roadway from San Francisco to New York.

When it was completed in 1936, Hoover Dam was praised as the Eighth Wonder of the World. The dam controlled the Colorado River, created the 115-mile (185-km)-long Lake Mead, and provided irrigation waters for 1 million acres (405,000 hectares) of farmland in three states. Its generators produced electricity for customers as far away as Los Angeles, California. Hoover Dam—the concrete colossus—changed life in the West forever.

Tourism, the New Bonanza

In Nevada's silver-mining era, playing cards and shooting dice were everyday activities. At various times, the state tried to outlaw gambling, but local sheriffs simply winked at back-room poker games. Finally lawmakers decided to legalize gambling in hopes of attracting out-of-state visitors.

The state legislature passed laws to legalize gambling in 1931. That same year, the legislature decreed that a married couple

Harold's Club

Nevada's first large-scale gambling house was Harold's Club, which opened in Reno in the late 1930s. Harold's Club was owned by Harold Smith, the son of a carnival operator. One feature at the club was a rodent run, where customers bet on mice that raced in a cage much as horses run on a track. Slot machines and card games at Harold's Club were honest, but the odds favored the house and customers lost huge sums of money. Still, crowds of people came to Harold's Club every day. ■

Benjamin "Don't Call Me Bugsy" Siegel

It was well-known that Nevada casinos took in fabulous amounts of cash, and hoodlums from around the country soon clamored for their share of this easy money. In 1946, gangster Benjamin Siegel began building the Flamingo Hotel and gambling casino in Las Vegas. Siegel murdered with such glee that other criminals called him

Bugsy, meaning "crazed." He hated the nickname and never let anyone use it to his face. Siegel's Flamingo Hotel was the most elaborate and expensive such facility ever built in Nevada. Siegel did not live to enjoy the gambling palace he created, however. Shortly after the Flamingo opened, he was gunned down in Los Angeles. ■

could be granted a divorce after having lived in Nevada for a period of six weeks. Other states required a year or more of residency before a divorce could be granted. Thus gambling and quick divorces were offered to attract out-of-staters. Nevada became known as the Sin State. A saying went, "If you can't do it at home, come to Nevada."

The Japanese bombing of Pearl Harbor in December 1941 sent the United States thundering into World War II (1939–1945). Nellis Air Force Base opened near Las Vegas and served as a gunnery school. Stead Air Force Base north of Reno trained radio operators. Now and then, U.S. leaders complained that Nevada's gambling halls were gobbling up the meager wages earned by soldiers, but the gambling continued without a break. Civilian employment soared during the war years. More than 2,000 workers held jobs at an ammunition depot near Hawthorne, while the city of Henderson had the nation's largest magnesium plant.

The population of Nevada jumped almost 50 percent from 1940 to 1950. More than half of this gain, however, went to two cities—Reno and Las Vegas. And with only 160,000 people in 1950, Nevada was still underpopulated.

Because the state had large tracts of uninhabited land, the federal government decided to use Nevada as a testing ground for atomic bombs. Starting in 1951, a series of 126 aboveground nuclear-weapons tests and 925 underground blasts were conducted at the Nevada Test Site in the southern part of the state. Some 10,000 people, many of them professional scientists, worked at the Nevada Test Site. Today Nevadans wonder whether the gain in

Eyewitness to a Bomb Blast

To simulate battle conditions, some atomic bombs were exploded aboveground with troops dug in near the blast site. Such a test took place in Nevada on April 15, 1955 (right). Forty years later, army officer John H. Vanston wrote about the experience in an article for *American Heritage* magazine: "As the time for the explosion approached, we all crouched in the bottom of our trenches with our hands over our eyes. . . . Then came a flash of unbelievable intensity. In the brilliant light I saw through my jacket—and through my arm—the pebbles at the bottom of the trench. I have recently learned that this is a real phenomenon, apparently caused by X rays induced by the explosion. . . . As I was recovering from the flash, the temperature changed from morning cold to the hottest day I could remember. Then the earth suddenly jumped to what I felt to be about 6 feet [1.8 m] in the air and then fell back and began to tremble violently. The thought rushed through my mind: They've miscalculated and blown up the whole world." ∎

jobs was worth the environmental damage the state suffered in those years of nuclear testing.

Nevada Today

Thousands of out-of-staters moved to Nevada in the 1960s and 1970s, and most established homes in Las Vegas and Reno. Las Vegas became one of the most exciting cities in the country. Fabulously rich gamblers from around the world vacationed in the city. Star entertainers such as Frank Sinatra, Dean Martin, Sammy Davis Jr., and Elvis Presley performed in Las Vegas's clubs and casinos.

Throughout the state, one out of three Nevadans worked for gambling businesses. In 1980, the average income of Nevadans was about $10,500 a year, seventh highest among the fifty states. But reliance on gambling to provide jobs came with a price. Nevada's rates of divorce, suicide, and alcoholism were far above those of other states.

The state government labored to get criminals out of the casino business by encouraging established businesses to buy the casinos. One such owner was Howard Hughes, who moved to Las Vegas in the late 1960s. Hughes was an eccentric millionaire who lived like a hermit in a Las Vegas hotel. When the hotel owner asked him to leave because several high-rolling gamblers wanted his suite of rooms, Hughes simply bought the hotel. Hughes also bought other casinos. During his buying sprees, Hughes chose Mormons to run his affairs. Mormons disapproved of gambling, drinking, and other Las Vegas vices, but the Mormon business-

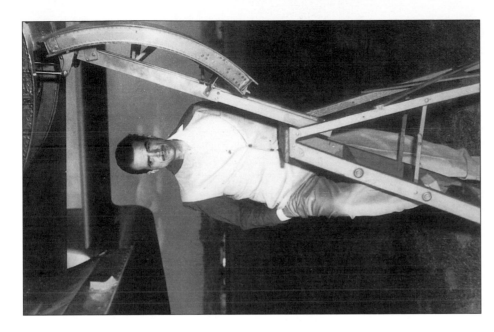

Millionaire Howard Hughes lived in Las Vegas.

men demanded that the clubs provide honest services for customers.

By 1990, the Las Vegas metropolitan area held almost 1 million people. Las Vegas remained a tourist center, but its image changed drastically as the city attempted to attract families as well as thrill-seeking gamblers. Slot machines were taken out of hotel hallways to please parents with small children. Even conservative church groups such as the Southern Baptists now hold conventions in Las Vegas.

Nuclear material and Nevada's wide-open spaces again became a controversial issue. In the 1990s, the federal government began to build a nuclear-waste burial site in Yucca Mountain, about 100 miles (161 km) northwest of Las Vegas. Workers dug a 1,400-acre (567-ha) complex of tunnels to hold the wastes. The massive project cost $2.2 billion and employed thousands of people. The site was supposed to receive nuclear waste from eighty reactors in forty-one states. But this waste material is dangerously radioactive and will remain that way for 10,000 years. Though the material was to be encased in metal and concrete cylinders, people feared that the cylinders could eventually leak and contaminate the air or the groundwater. Many Nevada politicians fought to keep the wastes out of their

state. U.S. senator Richard Bryan angrily declared, "[The federal government] want a toilet to flush their nuclear waste down. And that toilet is Nevada." Through the efforts of Bryan and others, the nuclear-waste storage plan has been delayed until at least 2010.

Tourism still provides the bulk of Nevada's jobs, but gambling is no longer the only attraction for visitors. Today's message is this: Nevada is a beautiful state, filled with delightful people. Appreciate Nevada for its God-given qualities.

Opposite: The Bellagio is one of Las Vegas's newest resorts.

CHAPTER FIVE

Sagebrush and Open Spaces

Sagebrush is the Nevada state flower.

...agebrush that rolled over the vast plateaus and brutal desert mountains like an endless desert sea, ringing the few scattered hamlets and towns of Nevada so that they were like the islands in that sea. Sagebrush growing down to the banks of rare streams and rivers. . . . Sagebrush giving up its domain only when it reached the foothills of the western Sierra where deep forests of pine and fir and tamarack ruled supreme."

—Robert Laxalt, in his book *Nevada: A Bicentennial History*

The Lay of the Land

Nevada spreads over 110,567 square miles (286,369 square kilometers), making it slightly smaller than the entire nation of Italy. Oregon and Idaho border it on the north. Its western border with California is shaped like a bow, with Lake Tahoe at the bow's

Opposite: The Valley of Fire

Nature's Sculptures

Windblown sand carves strikingly beautiful rock formations in parts of Nevada. At Valley of Fire State Park near the town of Overton, visitors can see bizarre rock formations with names such as Elephant Rock, Seven Sisters, and the Bee- hives. Cathedral Gorge State Park (left) near the city of Caliente is also a fantasyland of windblown figures. Stretch your imagination while visiting the park and you'll see cathedrals, wedding cakes, camels, and dragons. ■

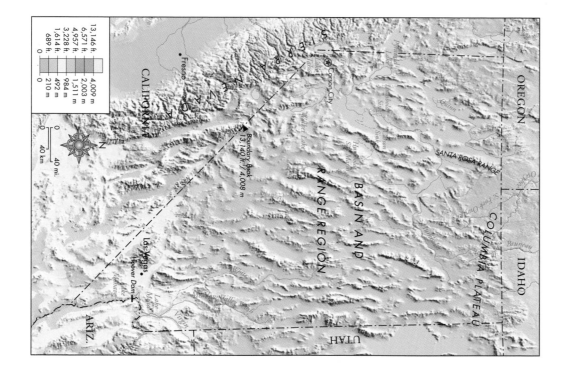

OREGON

IDAHO

COLUMBIA PLATEAU

SANTA ROSA RANGE

Bruneau

Owyhee

N E V A D A

BASIN AND RANGE REGION

CALIFORNIA

Fresno

Carson City

Boundary Peak
13,140 ft. / 4,008 m

Las Vegas
Hoover Dam
Lake Mead

ARIZ.

UTAH

13,146 ft.	4,009 m
6,571 ft.	2,003 m
4,957 ft.	1,511 m
3,228 ft.	984 m
1,614 ft.	492 m
689 ft.	210 m
0	0

N

0   40 mi.

0   40 km

The Great Basin National Park

The Great Basin National Park (right) spreads across eastern Nevada. Established in 1986, the 77,000-acre (31,185-ha) preserve is the only national park completely within Nevada's borders. (Parts of Death Valley National Park also lie in Nevada.) The park can be entered from the nearby city of Baker. It is home to sheep, mountain lions, deer, and elk. A high-light of the park is a forest of bristlecone pine trees that stand on the mountain peaks. Bristlecones are the oldest living things on earth, and many bristlecones in the park are 3,000 to 4,000 years old, which means they were saplings when the pyramids were built in Egypt. ■

peak. To the southeast, the Colorado River forms its border with Arizona, and Utah lies to the east.

The dominant land feature of Nevada is the Great Basin, a 200,000-square-mile (518,000-sq-km) desert region. The Great Basin is so named because the waters in its streams stay inside like water trapped in a bowl. Nevada lies in the heart of the Great Basin, which stretches into California, Idaho, Oregon, Utah, and Wyoming.

From the air, the Nevada portion of the Great Basin's surface looks like corrugated roof. More than 150 mountain ranges cross

Nuclear Scars

Few tourists visit the area on Yucca Flat that was once the sprawling grounds of the Nevada Test Site. At the height of the Cold War, about one atomic device a month was exploded there, making it by far the most heavily bombed place on earth. The site once held a boomtown—some called it a "doomtown"—where scientists and support staff worked. Radioactivity remains in the soil and some reports claim Yucca Flat is the most dangerous ground on earth. For years, people living downwind of the test site have suffered abnormally high cancer rates. ■

Wheeler Peak in Great Basin National Park

Nevada, mostly in a north-south direction. Most of these mountain ranges are between 5 to 15 miles (8 to 24 km) wide and anywhere from 50 to 75 miles (80 to 121 km) long. The ranges ripple like waves over the basin's surface at intervals of about 20 miles (32 km). Some of the mountains within Nevada's basin are higher than the basin's rims. Between the mountains lie buttes (hills that stand alone) and level valleys.

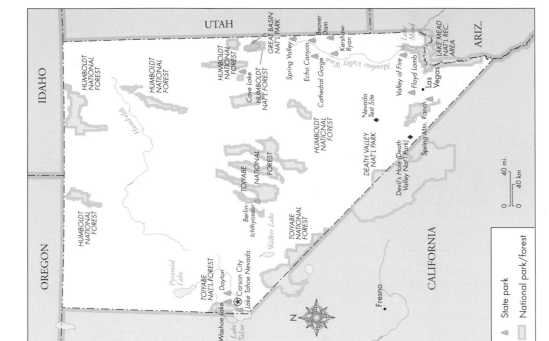

The lofty Sierra Nevada cut across the bow-shaped corner of Nevada near Lake Tahoe and Carson City. This is one of the few areas of Nevada that is not part of the Great Basin. Here are tall pines, mountain lakes, and snow-covered slopes that delight skiers. Nevada's highest mountain is Boundary Peak, which rises 13,140 feet (4,008 m) along its western border with California.

Climate

A general description of the Nevada climate is hot and dry. However the state is almost 500 miles (805 km) long, so Nevada has a wide range of temperatures. In southern Nevada, around Las Vegas, the summers are long and hot. Temperatures often exceed 110°F (43° Celsius) in the far south. Winters in the south are brief and mild. The north, on the other hand, has long cold winters. The desert is known for tremendous temperature shifts within a twenty-four-hour period. Temperatures in the deserts can rise to 100°F (38°C) during the day and then drop to near freezing at night. One of Nevada's greatest writ-

Nevada's parks and forests

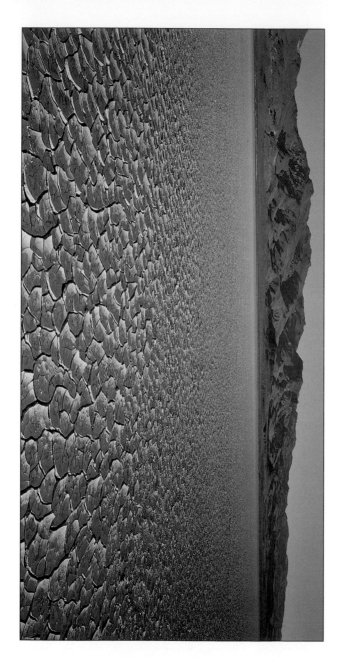

The cracked earth of Black Rock Desert

ers, Walter Van Tilburg Clark, wrote this satirical poem describing the climate of his home state:

So, the hills are in rows and they're piled up too high;
They are colder than death and they trouble the sky
Though at night you will freeze, yet at noon you will fry
In the unfinished land of Nevada.

Mountains create deserts. Nevada's desert-causing range is the Sierra Nevada on the western border. Clouds of wet air move inland from the Pacific Ocean and rise when they hit the great wall of the Sierras. The clouds then turn cool, can no longer hold their moisture, and dump most of their rain on the western (California) side of the Sierra Nevada range. By the time the clouds reach Nevada, they are high and dry and have little rain to spare.

Nevada's Geographical Features

Total area; rank	110,567 sq. mi. (286,369 sq km); 7th
Land; rank	109,806 sq. mi. (284,398 sq km); 7th
Water; rank	761 sq. mi. (1,971 sq km); 34th
Inland water; rank	761 sq. mi. (1,971 sq km); 28th
Geographic center	Lander, 26 miles (42 km) southeast of Austin
Highest point	Boundary Peak, 13,140 feet (4,008 m)
Lowest point	Colorado River in Clark County, 479 feet (146 m)
Largest city	Las Vegas
Population; rank	1,206,152 (1990 census); 39th
Record high temperature	122°F (50°C) at Overton on June 23, 1954; at Echo Bay on August 6, 1981; and at Echo Bay and Laughlin on August 8, 1985
Record low temperature	–50°F (–46°C) at San Jacinto on January 8, 1937
Average July temperature	73°F (23°C)
Average January temperature	30°F (–1°C)
Average annual precipitation	9 inches (23 cm)

Nevada averages only 9 inches (23 cm) of total precipitation (a combination of rain and snow) per year, making it the driest of all the fifty states. An exception to this pattern is the Sierra region, where annual rainfall averages 25 inches (64 cm) and mountain streams create the lovely Lake Tahoe.

Rivers and Lakes

Because of scant rains inland, Nevada's rivers would be called streams in other states. Some flow only in the wet season, which usually lasts from December to March. Most rivers empty into lakes or into low spots called sinks. The longest is the Humboldt River, which meanders about 300 miles (483 km) and ends in the

Lake Mead

Before Hoover Dam was built, the Colorado River wound through southern Nevada, sometimes slowing to a trickle and at other times flooding the land. Hoover Dam, finished in 1936, controlled this fickle river and created Lake Mead in the process. At its birth, Lake Mead was the largest human-made lake in the world.

Today, its 550 miles (885 km) of shoreline make Lake Mead a popular playground. Swimming and boating are fun-filled activities in the lake. Fishers pull in striped bass, some of which weigh 20 pounds (9 kg). Lake Mead sprawls over 245 square miles (635 sq km), making it the largest artificial lake in the Americas. ■

Humboldt Sink. The Carson River begins in the Sierras and empties into the Carson Sink. The Walker River also begins in the Sierra region and terminates in Walker Lake. The beautiful Truckee River flows out of Lake Tahoe, runs past the cities of Reno and Sparks, and then forms Pyramid Lake. To the south, the Virgin and Muddy Rivers join the Colorado River and eventually reach the sea.

Lake Tahoe is snuggled in the Sierras on the border with California. Roughly two-thirds of Lake Tahoe is in California, and the

A full moon over Lake Tahoe

A Modern Glacier

A glacier still exists in Nevada. A permanent ice field in the Great Basin National Park moves inch by inch over the land. The ice field is tiny compared to those in the far north, but its properties tell geologists that it is a genuine glacier. ■

The Joshua tree is one of the unique plants that grow in the desert.

remaining third lies in Nevada. Lake Tahoe is one of the world's deepest lakes. Pyramid Lake and Walker Lake are two other large bodies of water in western Nevada. Thousands of years ago, most of the western part of the state was covered by a huge lake that geologists call Lake Lahontan. That ancient lake dried up when the Ice Age ended, leaving Walker Lake and Pyramid Lake as reminders of the time when Nevada was a wet region.

Plants and Animals

Sagebrush is the most common plant in Nevada. A bushy plant, sagebrush grows anywhere from 1 to 12 feet (0.3 to 3.7 m) high. During long dry periods, sagebrush dries up and looks lifeless, but at the very hint of rain its leaves burst forth, and yellow or white flowers appear on its stems. Its wonderful ability to survive drought makes sagebrush Nevada's dominant plant.

Also growing in the deserts are Joshua trees, cacti, yuccas, and bushy plants known as shadscales. Grasslands along mountains and in valleys change color with the season. In the spring, the meadows explode with wildflowers such as the shooting star, white and yellow violets, and Indian paintbrush. Forests of fir and pine trees cover the Sierras on Nevada's western border. Other common trees include the aspen, the cottonwood, the hemlock, and the spruce.

The land of the Great Basin is usually treeless except for cottonwoods, which grow beside the basin's infrequent streams, and pines, which stand on its mountaintops. One early traveler commented, "If there is a state in North America where an active, experienced woodsman might perish, that state is Nevada." Actually that statement is an exaggeration because it is not true for all of Nevada. Lush green forests stand in the Sierras and in other areas.

A cottonwood tree in the Washoe Valley

The Wild Horse

Since the pioneer days, wild horses known as mustangs have roamed Nevada. These horses broke away from their owners and thrived in the sagebrush country. Over the years, cowboys tried to rope the mustangs and convert them into riding horses. Said one old cowboy, "For a saddlehorse, the mustangs . . . were tough. They would go forever without getting tired." Today, wild horses are protected, and an estimated 20,000 to 30,000 of them live in the state. Wild burros also live in Nevada. They, too, are descendants of animals that escaped from miners many years ago. ■

Large animals include the Rocky Mountain elk, the black bear, mule deer and the white-tailed deer, the pronghorn, and the bighorn sheep (the official state animal). Cottontail rabbits dart over grasslands. The deserts are home to rare creatures such as the Gila monster and the desert tortoise. Twenty-six varieties of lizards live in the state, the most common being the Western fence lizard.

Rare Fish in a Dry State

The Ice Age left Nevada largely a desert region, but several isolated lakes remain. Over thousands of years, unique fish evolved in those bodies of water. A large sucker called the cui-ui, found only in Pyramid Lake, is on the endangered wildlife list. A pond near the town of Death Valley Junction is home to the distinctive Devils Hole pupfish, which is also endangered. ■

An interesting reptile is the sidewinder, known for the S-shaped tracks it leaves in the desert sands. Trout, salmon, and whitefish swim in Nevada's rivers and lakes. Game birds include partridge and quail.

Hikers must beware of the seven types of rattlesnakes that inhabit Nevada. However, your chances of being bitten by a rattler are rare. In the past fifty years, only two deaths due to snakebites have occurred in the state.

CHAPTER SIX

Quiet Villages and Bright Lights

Gerlach is one of Nevada's small towns.

A lmost nine of every ten Nevadans live in cities or towns. Nevada's urban centers range from small mining or cattle-ranching villages to the glitter and bright lights of Reno and Las Vegas.

The North, Land of the Cowboys

The state officially calls its rugged northlands Cowboy Country. Some 150 years ago, settlers trekked along the Humboldt River in northern Nevada looking for inviting places to set up cattle and sheep ranches. U.S. Route 80 now parallels the Humboldt, and tourists can ride the highway to enjoy this historic region.

The north is a lonely country. Two of the biggest towns in the northwest part of the state are Gerlach and Empire. A Gerlach road sign lists its population as 350, but local people claim the true figure is smaller than that.

Opposite: The remains of a town in Death Valley

**The Pershing County
Courthouse in Lovelock**

Along the border with Oregon and Idaho are the small towns of Denio, McDermitt, Owyhee, and Jackpot. Denio is named for Aaron Denio, an Illinois pioneer who started ranching here in the 1860s. Owyhee is a mispronunciation of *Hawaii*. Long ago a group of Hawaiians bought land here, and for some reason the misnomer Owyhee became the name of the town and its major river. The small city of Jackpot is a gambling center, and there is no mystery why it is so named.

To the south is the town of Lovelock, with a pleasant and old-fashioned downtown section. Lovelock's Pershing County Courthouse is one of only two round courthouses in the United States.

Land Speed Record

North of Gerlach and Empire spreads the Black Rock Desert. It is unusual in that much of this desert has a hard-packed surface—almost as smooth as the floor of a gymnasium. This flatness makes the Black Rock Desert an ideal place to race super-high- speed cars. In 1997, a rocket-powered car called *Thrust II* thundered over the desert at the incredible speed of more than 760 mph (1,223 kph). It marked the first time in history that a ground vehicle exceeded the speed of sound. ■

Farther east along Route 80 is Winnemucca, named for a celebrated Paiute chief. Lovers of cowboy culture visit Winnemucca's Buckaroo Hall of Fame, where ranching tools and cowboy paintings are displayed.

In 1861, Indians attacked a wagon train and made off with cattle and other loot. The pioneers pursued the Indians, and a terrible battle broke out. Most of the fighting took place around a mountain later called Battle Mountain. A town of the same name grew on the mountain's crest. Today, Battle Mountain is a peaceful place, and tourists come to enjoy its fishing lake and its Olympic-size swimming pool.

Back in the 1950s, travel writer Lowell Thomas called Elko "the last real cow town in the American West." Elko retains much of its old cowboy charm. Classic Elko can be seen in its tree-shaded streets and its ninety-year-old courthouse. The town's shops display paintings and sculptures of the cowboy era. Elko is the biggest town in Cowboy Country, and it thrives on tourism and mining.

The Ruby Mountains

Toward the scenic village of Lamoille are the Ruby Mountains. This mountain range is sometimes called the Alps of Nevada. Many enjoy hiking the Ruby Crest National Recreation Trail past lakes, streams, and windswept mountain peaks. The complete Ruby Crest National Recreation Trail is 40 miles (64 km) long. To the north, near the town of Wells, is Ruby Marshes, a great spot for fishing. Nearby are Franklin Lake and the Lamoille Canyon. ■

Lake Tahoe and the Reno Region

Sitting like a diamond in the Sierras, Lake Tahoe is a spectacular body of water. Mark Twain once took a boat trip across the lake and said, "The bottom was so perfectly [clear] that the boat seemed to be floating in the air!" The towns of Incline Village, Glenbrook, Zephyr Cove, and Stateline serve as gateways to Lake Tahoe's 70 miles (113 km) of shoreline. Zephyr Cove is a busy winter resort, a favorite spot for skiers and snowmobile enthusiasts.

Lake Tahoe sits in the Sierra Nevada.

Virginia City is sometimes called the state's busiest ghost town. In the 1860s and 1870s, it was Nevada's wildest mining center. When its silver and gold were exhausted, Virginia City was largely abandoned, but it never quite lapsed into ghost-town status. Now the town entertains tourists with its history and a historic steam train. Its main street is lined with shops, museums, and Western-style saloons. Visitors walk the street and recall the days when Mark Twain said of rowdy Virginia City, "It was no place for a Presbyterian."

An excursion steam train for tourists in Virginia City

Reno was the state's original gambling spot when casinos were made legal in the 1930s. It remains a gambling city, but it offers visitors more than casinos. Reno's National Automobile Museum shows 200 antique and unusual cars. The Nevada Historical Society Museum, the state's oldest museum, displays items dating to prehistoric times. Thousands of visitors watch sky shows at Reno's Fleischmann Planetarium.

Just 1 mile (1.6 km) to the east is Sparks, Reno's sister city. In the 1940s and 1950s, while Reno gained fame as a gambling spot, Sparks established a reputation as a hard-working family-oriented town. This contrast led to an old joke: "Reno is so close to Hell, you can see Sparks." The city's downtown Victorian Square has attractive buildings dating to the 1890s. Sparks's Wild Island is northern Nevada's largest amusement complex.

Reno Information

Reno calls itself the Biggest Little City in the World, but it is actually the second biggest city in Nevada.

■ The city was named after Union general Jesse Lee Reno, a Civil War officer who was killed at the Battle of South Mountain.

■ The Truckee River runs through downtown Reno, and city leaders are justly proud of its two-block-long River Walk.

■ Reno has a special school, the Reno-Tahoe Gaming Academy, where men and women are taught how to become professional card dealers and get jobs in Nevada's casinos.

■ In 1910, Reno hosted a prizefight (right) called the Fight of the Century during which Jack Johnson, the first black heavyweight champion, defeated ex-champion James J. Jeffries. ■

Nevada history began in the Carson Valley. Genoa, which was founded by Mormons in 1851, is the oldest permanent non-Indian settlement in the state. The Genoa Courthouse Museum preserves relics of the state's past. Nearby are the Carson Valley towns of Minden and Gardnerville. An old high school building in Gardnerville houses the Carson Valley Museum and Cultural Center.

Carson City has been the capital since Nevada Territory was organized in 1861. The Nevada State Museum has life-size wax figures of Paiute Indians preparing food and

Downtown Carson City

The Carson Valley Curse

In 1857, the Mormon pioneers of the Carson Valley were ordered to return to Utah by their leader, Brigham Young. Mormon Orson Hyde dutifully obeyed. Before leaving, Hyde sold his sawmill for $10,000. The agreement stated that the buyer would pay most of the sum in the next year or so. The promised payment was never made, however. A furious Orson Hyde stood in the Utah legislature and cast a curse on all the peoples of the Carson Valley. Said Hyde, "You shall be visited of the Lord of Hosts with thunder and with earthquakes and with floods, with pestilence and with famine until your names are not known amongst men." The earthquakes and floods never came. The people of the Carson Valley did well, no doubt much to Hyde's displeasure. ◾

conducting their daily lives. The Stewart Indian Museum also displays Native American items. The Nevada capitol rises out of its own park, shaded by stately fir and maple trees. Completed in 1870, the capitol serves as a museum as well as a working meeting hall for the legislature. Inside are the wineglasses used by territorial governor James Nye to toast Nevada's statehood in 1864.

Riding the Pony Express Road

The state calls its central region Pony Express Territory. In the 1860s, fearless pony riders raced across the breadth of Nevada to bring mail to isolated western pioneers. U.S. Route 50 retraces the old Pony Express Trail. The modern highway also brings history to visitors.

Begin your journey through Western history at the city of Fallon. Ancient history is here too. Fallon was a hunting ground for

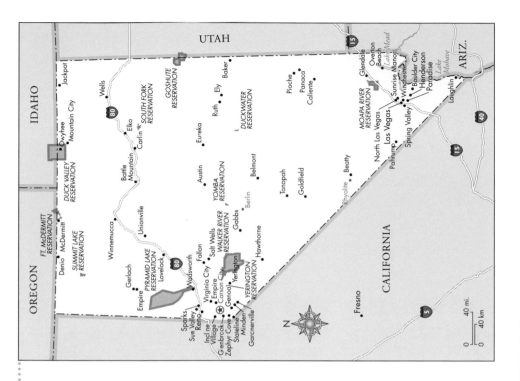

Nevada's cities and interstates

prehistoric people who left rock pictures at various places, including the nearby Hickison Petroglyph Site. But in Fallon you cannot escape the future. You'll hear a roar in the sky, look up, and see the latest navy jets streaking over the horizon. Fallon is the headquarters of the U.S. Navy's famous Top Gun flight school.

Austin once held some 10,000 people and was the state's second-largest city. But when the silver ran out, so did most of the people. Today, Austin's population is about 400. Visitors enjoy the town's remarkably well-preserved buildings. Austin's Catholic church is the oldest in the state. Its Methodist church has been in use every Sunday since 1866. Austin also has the distinction of being 12 miles (19 km) from the exact geographic center of Nevada.

Pony Express Trail

Near Fallon stand the ruins of a Pony Express station. Small stations, which were little more than sheds holding horses, stood 10 to 15 miles (16 to 24 km) apart along the Pony Express route. A rider galloped to the station carrying a leather pouch stuffed with letters. In less than thirty seconds, the rider hopped off his old horse, jumped on a fresh horse, and thundered on to the next station.

Mine ruins in Berlin

Travelers need a full tank before driving Route 50 through central Nevada; there aren't many gas stations. Years ago *Life* magazine called the Nevada portion of Route 50 the Loneliest Road in America. It retains that title now, as highway signs attest. Some say that twenty cars a day over Route 50 constitute a traffic jam.

It is appropriate that America's loneliest road should cut through a ghost town or two. Near the modern and very much alive town of Gabbs are the ruins of an older, long-abandoned small city. Berlin is said to be the best-preserved ghost town in Nevada. It was founded in 1863 and abandoned in the early 1900s. A state park was established in the area in 1955, and park rangers give tours of this one-time silver-mining village that dashed the dreams of its founders.

The word *eureka* is Greek for "I have found it!" It suggests excitement and the thrill of discovery. What a perfect name for a mining town. At one point Eureka rivaled Austin as a silver and gold producer. Today, the town is famed for its ornate opera house, built in 1880 and restored in 1994. The Eureka County Courthouse, with its pressed tin ceilings, is also worth a visit.

Railroad buffs gather at Ely to see the Nevada Northern Railway Museum. A highlight of a museum visit is a ride on a coal-fired 1910 steam locomotive called the Ghost Train of Old Ely. Most of the guides and people who run this historic train are former railroad workers. To the north is McGill, a tidy town that was once a copper producer. Baker and the Great Basin National Park lie to the east.

Pioneer Territory

State officials call the southern portion of Nevada, excluding the Las Vegas region, Pioneer Territory. Here, old mining towns stand alongside prosperous ranches. Most of the region's villages were started in the pioneer era, and all have stories to tell.

In the 1870s, citizens of Greenfield changed the name of their tiny town to Yerington in honor of H. M. Yerington, the owner of the Virginia & Truckee Railroad. The citizens hoped the name change would persuade Yerington to run a railroad track through their town. Mr. Yerington never complied, but the town grew anyway.

The Mizpah Hotel in Tonopah in 1907

Yerington's Lyon County Museum traces the history of the region over the last 130 years.

Hawthorne sits on the southern tip of Walker Lake. The town's Mineral County Museum displays mining equipment, antique cars, and Victorian clothing. The nearby village of Aurora had a gold-mining heyday, but it has been barely surviving for the past 100 years or so. Place names of land features close to Aurora reflect its mining past—Anchorite Hills, Whisky Flat, and Lucky Boy Pass.

Round Mountain has a unique children's playground. A resident of the town bought up dozens of huge tires used on mining trucks and buried them halfway into the sand to create a fun obstacle course for kids to crawl through. In the heat of the day, however, the playground is little used because rattlesnakes sometimes curl up in the tires.

Tonopah was a rip-roarin' Wild West town in the 1870s. One of its most successful card players and saloon operators—and its deadliest gunfighter—was Wyatt Earp. As students of Western history know, Earp later became a deputy U.S. marshal in Tombstone, Arizona, and participated in the famous battle at the O.K. Corral. Today, Tonopah is an energetic town, proud of its past. A grand parade complete with marching bands celebrates Tonopah's history during the city's Jim Butler Days festivities.

The tourist town of Beatty is a stopover for people eager to see spectacular desert scenery. A short drive from Beatty is the Nevada portion of Death Valley National Park, the rugged desert that spreads into California. The city of Pahrump to the south has a unique industry—it is the only place in Nevada where wine is made. *Pahrump* is a Shoshone Indian word meaning "deep waters." Springs in the region provide irrigation water to grow grapes, and the grapes are processed into wine.

Underground springs turned the towns of Alamo, Ash Springs, and Warm Springs into farming and ranching centers. To the northeast is Pioche, a quiet little community with a scandalous

Rugged Bouncer

In the early 1900s, everyone behaved properly in the barroom of Tonopah's Mizpah Hotel. The bar employed a no-nonsense bouncer named Jack Dempsey, who went on to become the heavyweight champion of the world. ■

Great Ghosts

Nevada has many ghost-town aficionados, people who travel up and down the state exploring abandoned settlements. High on the list for ghost-town fans is Rhyolite, which lies near Beatty. In 1907, Rhyolite (above) had 12,000 people, four newspapers, four banks, and an opera house. By 1920, when the ore was gone, the city was virtually empty. Today, Rhyolite is one of the most photographed ghost towns in Nevada. ■

past. Pioche is the home of "the Million Dollar Courthouse." The courthouse building is an interesting historical structure, but surely couldn't be worth its $1-million price tag. In truth the courthouse was built in 1871 for a budget of $26,000. Corrupt politicians drove the price up to nearly $1 million and pocketed the excess dollars.

Caliente was once a railroad crossroads, and its most spectacular building was a depot built in the style of a Spanish mission. The depot, constructed in 1923, is now the pride of Caliente and houses an art museum and a library. Panaca was founded by Mormons, whose church remains the social center of the town. By contrast, Pioche was created by rough-and-tumble miners. Murder was so frequent in Pioche's early days that it is said the town cemetery held almost fifty graves, none of which were occupied by men who died of natural causes. Today, Pioche's nineteenth-century buildings are historical gems.

Las Vegas Country

More than 60 percent of all Nevadans live in Clark County, home of Las Vegas, on the state's southern tip. Clark County enjoyed about a 5 percent increase in population each year during the 1990s. County leaders say the demand for workers in their region is double the national average.

Boulder City is the only town in the state where there is no casino gambling. Instead, Boulder City's biggest attraction is Hoover Dam. Visit the dam, stand on its 726-foot (221-m)-high top, and try to imagine the problems faced by the workers build-

The *Desert Princess* on Lake Mead

ing this monolith. Picture men dangling from cliffs on ropes like spiders as they drilled holes in the rock face to set explosives. Finally, take a trip on the *Desert Princess*, a paddlewheel tour boat that sails Lake Mead, the magnificent body of water created by the huge dam.

The city of North Las Vegas is an industrial center that celebrates Fairshow, an exhibition of hot-air balloons every autumn. During Fairshow, balloons of all sizes and colors fill the skies over

Hot-air balloons provide a spectacular sight in North Las Vegas.

the Las Vegas Valley. To the south is Henderson, the state's third-largest city. Henderson bloomed in World War II when some 5,000 men and women worked at the town's huge magnesium plant. The plant closed in 1944, and Henderson declined. But new industries have moved in, and Henderson is once again an important factory center.

When people who have not visited Las Vegas for twenty years return, they universally say, "How this place has grown!" Twenty years from now, returning tourists will probably still be in awe at how the place has expanded, or at least changed. Las Vegas has a way of reinventing itself every decade or so. Ten-story hotels are replaced by twenty-story hotels, which are then torn down to build forty-story hotels. Las Vegas is the greatest boomtown in Nevada's history of boomtown.

Las Vegas is a tourist giant with a dozen of the world's biggest hotels. Gambling remains the big lure. Hotels and casinos house slot-machine rooms that are bigger than football fields. Thousand-dollar bets roll over card and dice tables with such frequency that few people even notice. Gambling establishments like to entice the big gamblers, the so-called high rollers. But the poor lose money too, giving rise to one of the city's many nicknames—Lost Wages.

Everything is an exaggeration in Las Vegas. Hotels are not merely hotels—they are pleasure palaces. Guests of the Mirage Hotel enter an indoor rain forest. They hear a deep rumble and feel

The rain forest inside the Mirage Hotel

Kids and Gambling Don't Mix

Children are allowed to walk through a casino with their parents. The emphasis is on the word *through*. Children, even those accompanied by their parents or by other adults, are forbidden to stand or in any way loiter in a gambling hall. Security guards will order underage people to leave a gambling facility if they try to violate rules. Nevada law says you must be twenty-one years old to enter a casino on your own. ■

the floor tremble under their feet. From all sides come the sounds of jungle animals chirping in excitement. Then it happens: A volcano erupts, complete with fire, steamy water, and artificial lava.

Other hotels have other spectacles. The Bellagio features a formation of fountains and an 8-acre (3.2-ha) lake. The Excalibur harks back to the days of King Arthur and entertains guests with a jousting tournament. The Luxor has a life-size model of the Egyptian sphinx at its front entrance. Treasure Island presents a sea battle between two full-size sailing ships, staged right on the hotel's front lawn.

This is Las Vegas, a bizarre but exciting fantasyland.

Opposite: Pirates go to battle several times a day at Treasure Island.

CHAPTER SEVEN

Governing the Silver State

Inside the capitol

Opposite: The state capitol in Carson City

Nevada applied for statehood in 1864. To gain statehood, its constitution had to be on file in Washington, D.C. This presented a problem for the people in isolated Nevada. There was no railroad, and sending the written version of the constitution to the nation's capital via wagon train could take months. A telegraph line did run through Nevada, however, so a telegraph operator bent over his key and carefully clicked off every word of the constitution to Washington. This dot-and-dash operation cost $3,416.77, an enormous expense for the pioneer state. But Nevadans were eager to join the Union.

State Government at Work

Nevada is still governed by its 1864 constitution. The constitution provides rules for government. It divides state government into three branches or departments: the executive, the legislative, and the judicial. The executive department is charged with enforcing laws, the legislative branch creates new laws and rescinds old ones, and the judicial department hears cases and interprets the wording of the constitution. In theory, each branch acts as a watchdog over the others so that no one branch has too much power. The federal government of the United States is structured in the same manner.

Nevada's natural resources

What Nevada Grows, Manufactures, and Mines

Agriculture
Barley
Beef cattle
Hay
Potatoes
Wheat

Manufacturing
Fabricated metal
    products
Food products
Machinery
Printed materials
Transportation
    equipment

Mining
Gold
Silver

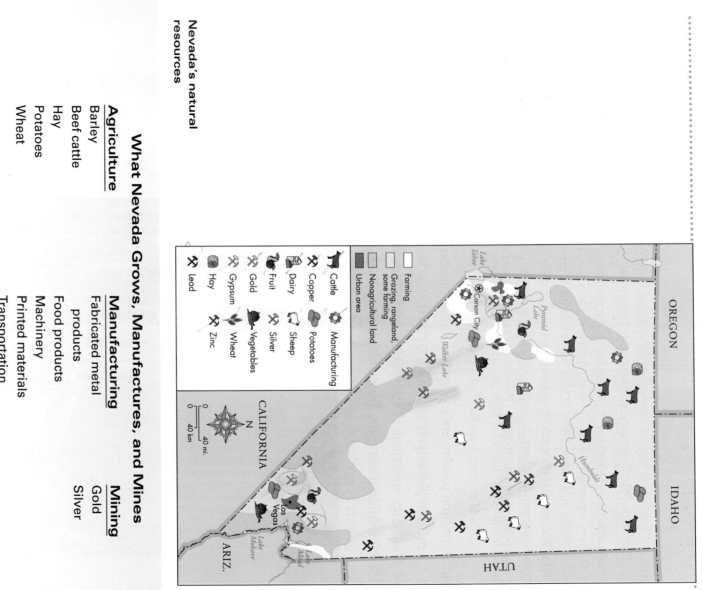

Legend:
- Urban area
- Nonagricultural land
- Grazing, rangeland, some farming
- Farming

- Cattle
- Copper
- Dairy
- Fruit
- Gold
- Gypsum
- Hay
- Lead
- Manufacturing
- Potatoes
- Sheep
- Silver
- Vegetables
- Wheat
- Zinc

OREGON

IDAHO

CALIFORNIA

ARIZ.

UTAH

Lake Tahoe
Pyramid Lake
Carson City
Walker Lake
Humboldt
Las Vegas
Lake Mohave
Lake Mead

N
0 40 mi.
0 40 km

Review-Journal, the *Las Vegas Sun*, and the *Reno Gazette Journal*. The magazine *Nevada*, which is published by the state government, is an excellent source of information about the Silver State. About seventy radio stations and fifteen television stations are active in Nevada. The state's first TV station, KOLO-TV, began in Reno in 1953.

Agriculture and Mining

Some 3,000 farms operate in Nevada. Small family farms are the norm. Half of the state's farms are less than 70 acres (28 ha). Wheat, hay, potatoes, and barley are the chief crops. Nevada's dry conditions discourage large-scale farming. The state's farms rank forty-seventh among the fifty states in total production, and less than 1 percent of Nevada's workers are employed in agriculture.

Nevada has about 1,700 cattle ranches. More than 500,000 head of cattle and 80,000 sheep and lambs graze on its grasslands. Cattle and sheep ranching are concentrated in the northeast. White Pine, Lander, Humboldt, Eureka, and Elko Counties are prime areas for ranching.

Mining is Nevada's number-two industry, after tourism. Nevada remains the leading gold producer of the fifty states. About two-thirds of all the gold mined in the United States comes from Nevada, and the total output of the state's gold mines makes the United States the world's second-largest gold producer, behind South Africa. The most productive gold mine is north of the city of Carlin in Elko County. Gold mines are also found in Eureka and Lander Counties. Nevada is also the nation's largest producer of silver. Most silver mines are found in the southwestern part of the

state. The city of Hawthorne is a leading silver center. Diatomite, which is used to make water filters, is another important mineral found in Nevada.

Precious metals, such as gold and silver, are subject to price changes on the world market. Through most of the 1990s, the price of gold was at or below $300 per ounce (31 grams). At this low price, many marginal mines could not make a profit, and the mining companies were forced to lay off workers. Though Nevada's gold and silver mines are rich with ore, mining employs less than 2 percent of the workforce.

Opposite: Cattle grazing in Carson Valley

CHAPTER NINE

A Look at Nevadans

A plant worker

he true wealth of a state lies not with its minerals or its factories but with its people. Nevada has an expanding population, and its people are excited about their future.

Come One, Come All

Nevada has been the nation's fastest-growing state since 1960. In the 1980s alone, the state gained 6,000 residents a week. From 1991 to 1996, another 400,000 people moved to the state. Clark County, which includes Las Vegas, increased in population by more than 350 percent from 1975 to 2000.

Studies show that in the 1990s only 20 percent of Nevada residents were born in the state. Of all the fifty states, Nevada has the lowest percentage of native-born people. Almost one-third of the newly arriving residents come from California.

Opposite: Fishing at Lake Tahoe

Opposite: Most of Nevada remains unpopulated.

Plentiful jobs lure young people to Nevada. Retired folks are attracted to its mild, if often very hot, climate. Still others come to enjoy the nightlife, the gambling, and the glitz and glitter that Las Vegas and the casinos offer.

The casino lifestyle, with its emphasis on gambling and drinking, contributes to acute health problems. The average Nevadan drinks almost 5 gallons (19 liters) of alcohol a year, the highest rate in the nation. Largely because of alcohol consumption, Nevada is among the top ten states in traffic fatalities. One of every three adults in Nevada smokes, and the state ranks high in smoking-related deaths. Nevada leads the nation in suicides. These negative statistics are inflated by people who come to Nevada for the wrong reasons. For those who avoid the excesses the casinos offer, Nevada is a healthy environment.

Perspectives on the People

Despite the state's amazing growth, Nevada is still underpopulated. Though the state has enjoyed great percentage gains in recent years, it started with a low population base. In 1950, Nevada had only 160,000 people. Fifty years later, its population had increased tenfold, but Nevada still ranked among the fifteen least populous states. Also, Nevadans are concentrated in cities and towns, so there are plenty of wide-open spaces left in the Silver State.

In terms of size, Nevada ranks seventh among the fifty states. But in 1990, it had more than 1.2 million residents, thirty-ninth among the states in population. Nevada's population density is 11

Population of Nevada's Major Cities (1990)

Las Vegas	258,295
Reno	133,850
Paradise	124,682
Sunrise Manor	95,362
Henderson	64,942
Sparks	53,367

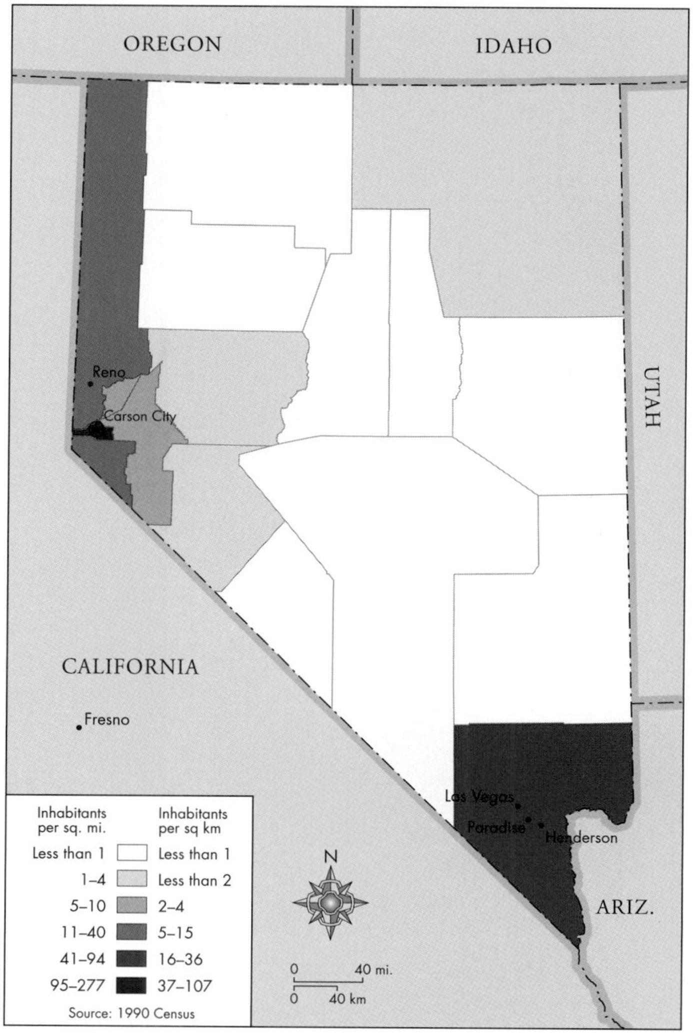

Nevada's population density

Inhabitants per sq. mi.

Less than 1
1–4
5–10
11–40
41–94
95–277

Inhabitants per sq km

Less than 1
Less than 2
2–4
5–15
16–36
37–107

Source: 1990 Census

N

0   40 mi.
0   40 km

persons per square mile (4 per sq km), while the national average is 69 persons per square mile (27 per sq km). This emptiness leaves much of Nevada with an untouched and unspoiled atmosphere that lovers of nature appreciate.

Close to 90 percent of Nevadans live in city areas. Only Cali-

Wovoka

One of the state's most important Native Americans was a Paiute named Wovoka (1858?–1932), who was born near Walker Lake. Wovoka was indirectly responsible for history's last battle between Indians and U.S. soldiers. When Wovoka was fourteen, his father died, and he went to work for a white rancher. He learned Christianity but never forgot his old religion. In 1889, Wovoka had a powerful religious vision. He saw Native Americans rising up—some even from the dead—to reclaim their ancient lands. Wovoka told other Indian peoples to participate in a special Ghost Dance that would bring spirits from their graves. They should also wear Ghost Shirts (shirts with painted religious symbols) to protect them from bullets. Chief Sitting Bull and the Sioux people of South Dakota embraced Wovoka's vision with particular zeal. The result was the Wounded Knee Massacre of 1890, a terrible battle where U.S. soldiers killed about 200 Indian men, women, and children. ∎

fornia, New Jersey, and Hawaii have a greater percentage of urban dwellers. Las Vegas is by far the largest city in the state. The Reno-Sparks region is the second-largest urban area.

Through much of its history, Nevada was home to white pioneers and Native American peoples. Migration has changed that

The Basques

They arrived more than 100 years ago and began sheep ranching in northern Nevada. They were the Basques, an ancient European ethnic group. Though the Basques came from the Pyrenees between France and Spain, they never considered themselves to be Spanish or French.

Some legends claim they were the survivors of the lost continent of Atlantis. In addition to sheep ranching, the Basques established hotels and restaurants in northern Nevada towns. There they danced, ate, and talked of old times. The Basque restaurants remain, and they serve hearty meals of soup, salad, beans, and lamb chops. ∎

Basque Garlic Soup

Every summer, descendants of Basque immigrants celebrate their heritage at the National Basque Festival in Elko. No visit to the Elko area is complete without a trip to one of the Basque restaurants to try one of their traditional dishes, such as garlic soup.

Ingredients:

Olive oil
6 cloves of garlic, sliced
1/2 cup parsley, chopped
water
3 eggs

Directions:

Coat the bottom of a large skillet with oil. Heat the oil, and add the garlic. Stir the garlic in the skillet until it turns a golden brown. Add the parsley and enough water to cover the parsley, and fill the skillet up to about 3/4 inch from the top.

Bring the water to a boil, reduce the heat and simmer for 15 minutes. Carefully add the eggs one at a time. You can stir the eggs into the soup or poach them by just dropping them into the soup and allowing them to cook through.

Simmer for an additional 5 minutes or until the eggs are done.

picture. Nevada is now 84.26 percent white, 10.35 percent Hispanic, 6.55 percent African-American, and 3.17 percent Asian American. Native Americans, the original inhabitants of the state, now make up only 1.63 percent of the population.

The religions practiced in Nevada reflect the diversity of the people. In 1990, the state had more than 150,000 Roman Catholics,

St. Mary's in the Mountains Church in Virginia City

about 90,000 Mormons, 27,000 Southern Baptists, 20,400 Jews, and 6,000 Lutherans. Nevadans are churchgoing people despite the temptations of the casinos. Some reports say there are more churches per capita in Las Vegas—Sin City—than in any other city in the nation.

Education

Early in its history, Nevada's schools were hampered by a small population and the great distances that pupils and teachers had to travel. One-room schools that served grades one through eight were common. Many of these one-room schools had only ten to twenty students. Money to support the school systems was scarce. In Carson City in the 1860s, money for schools came from what was called a Rowdy Fund. When drunken cowboys or miners got into fights or destroyed property, they were made to pay into the Rowdy Fund, which was then used to pay teachers and buy books.

The University of
Nevada at Reno

Today, all Nevada children between ages seven and seventeen are required to attend school. More than 200,000 students are enrolled in the state's public schools. In the mid-1990s, Nevada taxpayers spent $5,100 per year per student to maintain the state school system.

Some 82 percent of Nevada's population are high school graduates. Yet Nevada has one of the nation's highest school-dropout rates. Each year about one in seven children stops attending classes before finishing high school.

Nevada has two major universities: the University of Nevada, with campuses in Las Vegas and Reno, and Sierra Nevada College in Incline Village. About 20,000 students study at the Las Vegas campus of the University of Nevada, and some 12,000 attend the Reno branch. The Mackay School of Mines, one of the world's finest institutions dedicated to training mine engineers, is located on the Reno campus of the University of Nevada.

CHAPTER TEN

Entertainment and Fine Arts

Reno hosts Hot August Nights, a celebration of classic cars and rock 'n' roll.

Nevadans are proud of their culture. Theirs is a Western state, full of the poetry of the pioneer era. Music, sports, and a passion for festivals consume the people.

The Festive People

Why wait for a major event such as Christmas or New Year's Eve to hold a party? People of the Silver State don't wait. They will use any occasion to throw a bash.

Offbeat festivals are common in Nevada. Consider Wells, a normally quiet village in the north. During the first part of each year, the town's tranquillity is shattered as tiny Wells imitates mighty Rome by holding a chariot race down its main street. The town of Battle Mountain relives its past every April with the Easter Pow-

Opposite: The Great Reno Balloon Race

Entertainment and Fine Arts **117**

wow—an event that brings Native Americans and the sons and daughters of settlers together. Laughlin's Harley Days in April attract lovers of classic Harley-Davidson motorcycles. Tonopah's Jim Butler Days feature arm-wrestling competitions.

Nevadans honor their colorful history in festivals. The Carson City Rendezvous harks back to the state's exploration period by displaying typical camps used by the Mountain Men. Food, music, and crafts abound during Beatty's Railroad Days festival. The Spirit of Wovoka Days Powwow, held at Yerington, recalls the mystical Paiute chief and the spirit-raising Ghost Dance. The Silver State celebrates its statehood every October 31 in Carson City.

Nevada's diverse population gives a special flavor to ethnic celebrations. Firecrackers and paper dragons herald the Chinese New Year in Las Vegas. Also in Las Vegas is the yearly Mariachi Festival, a favorite of the Mexican community. The Reno Basque celebration features a contest called Irrintzi, in which contestants outdo each other by uttering the loudest and longest yells. The Dr. Martin Luther King Jr. Birthday Celebration is a four-day observance of civil rights held every January in Reno and Sparks. Native American dancers, drummers, and singers perform every March at the Stewart Indian Museum in Carson City for the Annual Mother Earth Awakening Powwow.

Arts and Literature

Art in Nevada has a history that began almost 10,000 years ago when unknown Indian artists carved pictures on the faces of rocks. Centuries later, Nevada Indians retain a love of arts and crafts. A Washo woman named Dat-So-La-Lee, who died in 1925 at the age of ninety-six, was perhaps the most famous basketmaker in the world. One of her baskets was displayed at the Carnegie Museum in Pittsburgh, Pennsylvania, where it was hailed as a magnificent work of art.

Painters came and went during Nevada's pioneer era. Some painters were down-on-their-luck miners who painted pictures on the walls of taverns to earn a few dollars. The best examples of this saloon art were bought up and carried away by rich Californians. The Latimer Art Club, formed in Reno in 1921, was the first of its kind in the state. The club's founder was California artist Lorenzo P. Latimer, and for many years it was the only art society in the state. However, the world of painting and sculpture soon mush-

The Latimer Art Club in 1924

Sarah Winnemucca Hopkins

roomed. Painter Robert Caples (1908–1979) became celebrated for his murals, or wall paintings, and charcoal drawings of Nevada Indians. One of Caples's most striking murals is in the lobby of the Washoe County Courthouse. By the 1990s, more than 200 arts organizations were flourishing in Nevada.

The art scene today focuses on Las Vegas and its exciting art exhibitions. Cherished paintings and sculptures are displayed in Las Vegas hotels on a come-and-go basis as if these traveling art shows were visiting bands. One Las Vegas hotel has a high-priced restaurant called the Picasso, where more than thirty-five paintings and drawings by the famous artist Pablo Picasso are on permanent display. Another hotel has a Venetian theme, and re-creates the art treasures of Venice, Italy. In most communities artworks are housed in museums, but Las Vegas, of course, is a different city. There, the casino hotels are showcases for paintings and sculpture.

Literature also has deep roots in Nevada. Sarah Winnemucca Hopkins (1844?–1891) was the daughter of the Paiute chief Winnemucca. She married a U.S. Army officer, learned the English language, and wrote *Life Among the Paiutes: Their Wrongs and Claims*. Hop-

Pioneer Opera

Music and drama were a welcome relief to dreary mining-camp life. Early shows were put on in tents. Later, Comstock boomtowns built their own opera houses where plays, concerts, and full-scale operas were performed. Often these entertainment halls were the finest buildings in town. Virginia City, Gold Hill, and Carson City had the most luxurious opera houses in Nevada's pioneer days. The state's own opera star was Emma Nevada (1859–1946). Born Emma Wixon near Austin, she toured the United States and Europe as one of the greatest opera performers of her time. Emma changed her last name to Nevada to honor her home state. ■

Walter Van Tilburg Clark

kins's book is a fascinating account of Indian life before Europeans came to Nevada.

Mark Twain (1835–1910) was the most prominent writer to live in Nevada during the pioneer era. Twain's book *Roughing It* tells exciting and often hilarious tales of his travels among miners, card players, and various lowlifes in the Comstock area. At one point, Twain tried his hand at mining but discovered only mica, a glittering mineral the old-timers called fool's gold. Twain wrote of his disappointment, "So vanished my dream. So melted my wealth away. . . . Moralizing, I observed, then, that 'all that glisters is not gold.'"

Walter Van Tilburg Clark (1909–1971) wrote the best-selling *The Ox-Bow Incident* (1943), a compelling story about a posse that is intent on hanging a gang of men suspected of murder and cattle-rustling. The question looms: Does the posse have the right men? Clark was a professor at the University of Nevada, and his novel became a hit movie in the 1940s. Robert Laxalt (1921–), who grew up in Nevada, wrote *Sweet Promised Land*. The book is a charming tale of the author's father, who came to Nevada from the Basque district of Spain.

Robert Laxalt also wrote *Nevada: A Bicentennial History*. Laxalt is from a prominent Nevada family. His brother, Paul, served as Nevada's governor from 1967 to 1971 and as U.S. senator from Nevada from 1975 to 1987.

The Shakespeare Festival at Sand Harbor

Every August the powerful works of William Shakespeare are performed in the Lake Tahoe region. This award-winning summer festival takes place at Sand Harbor in Incline Village. ■

The annual Cowboy Poetry Gathering held every January in Elko is a Nevada literary tradition. Here, genuine cowboys, true riders of the range, tell of life as they see it. Loneliness, joy, despair—all are subjects for cowboy poems. One by one, the cowboys at Elko recite their lines before entranced audiences. Some pluck a guitar and spin their poems to music.

Sports

There are no major professional sports teams in Nevada. Fans follow the exploits of the University of Nevada at Las Vegas (UNLV) basketball team, the Running Rebels. The state went wild in 1990 when UNLV won the men's college basketball championship.

With the opening of the Las Vegas Motor Speedway in 1996, Nevada became one of the world's top auto-racing destinations. Nicknamed the Diamond in the Desert, this complex hosts all sorts of races, from go-karts to major NASCAR races. The speedway seats more than 250,000 people for major events, such as the Las Vegas 400.

Skiing is a passion in the Silver State. Few places offer skiers such variety—steep powder chutes, open bowls, and tree skiing. The Sierras near Reno are home to thirteen cross-country ski areas and fifteen downhill ski resorts, including Squaw Valley, the site

Skiing at Squaw Valley

The Silver State offers many ways to enjoy the outdoors.

of the 1960 Winter Olympic Games. Lake Tahoe has an annual snowfall of about 350 inches (889 cm), ideal for winter sports. Skiing is also popular in the Ruby Mountains to the east.

There are more than sixty golf courses in Nevada. Las Vegas alone has twenty golf courses, and Reno has ten. The Las Vegas International Golf Tournament, held in October, draws the world's top golfers. The Reno Rodeo, held every June, is billed as the Wildest, Richest Rodeo in the West. The town of Winnemucca hosts the U.S. Team Roping Championship, where some 3,000 teams of cowboys from all over the West compete for prizes.

Nevada's wild countryside is ideal for outdoor sports and activities. Families and groups enjoy pedaling mountain bikes through the state's rugged high country. Fishing enthusiasts travel hundreds of miles to fly-fish in Nevada's streams. Swimming and waterskiing are popular in Lake Mead. Thousands of miles of hiking trails wind through the state parks.

Its lively sports and entertainment scene draws many people to the Silver State. Visitors soon discover why Nevada is the fastest-growing state in the nation. It is a wonderful land, filled with friendly people.

Timeline

United States History

1607 The first permanent English settlement is established in North America at Jamestown.

1620 Pilgrims found Plymouth Colony, the second permanent English settlement.

1776 America declares its independence from Britain.

1783 The Treaty of Paris officially ends the Revolutionary War in America.

1787 The U.S. Constitution is written.

1803 The Louisiana Purchase almost doubles the size of the United States.

1812-15 The United States and Britain fight the War of 1812.

1861-65 The North and South fight each other in the American Civil War.

Nevada State History

1776 Francisco Garcés, a Spanish priest, is the first European to see Nevada.

1848 Nevada is ceded to the U.S. by Mexico.

1851 First permanent settlement is founded by Mormans in Genoa.

1859 Silver is discovered in western Nevada, creating a rush to the area.

1861 Nevada Territory is created by the U.S. government.

1864 Nevada becomes the thirty-sixth state on October 31.

1890 As the demand for silver decreases, Nevada suffers a severe population drop.

Nevada State History

1931 Gambling is legalized by the state legislature. The state also allows couples living in Nevada for only six weeks to obtain divorces.

1936 Hoover Dam is completed.

1951 The U.S. government begins testing atomic weapons in Nevada.

1980 State legislators pass the Lake Tahoe antipollution bill.

United States History

1917–18 The United States is involved in World War I.

1929 The stock market crashes, plunging the United States into the Great Depression.

1941–45 The United States fights in World War II.

1945 The United States becomes a charter member of the U.N.

1951–53 The United States fights in the Korean War.

1964 The U.S. Congress enacts a series of groundbreaking civil rights laws.

1964–73 The United States engages in the Vietnam War.

1991 The United States and other nations fight the brief Persian Gulf War against Iraq.

Fast Facts

Nevada state
capitol

Sagebrush

Statehood date	October 31, 1864, the 36th state
Origin of state name	Spanish for "snow covered"
State capital	Carson City
State nicknames	Silver State, Sagebrush State, and Battle Born State
State motto	All for Our Country
State bird	Mountain bluebird
State flower	Sagebrush
State fish	Lahontan cutthroat trout
State animal	Desert bighorn sheep
State reptile	Desert tortoise

State fossil	Ichthyosaur
State rock	Sandstone
State gemstone	Black fire opal
State metal	Silver
State song	"Home Means Nevada"
State trees	Bristlecone pine and single-leaf piñon
State grass	Indian ricegrass
State fair	Reno, in August
Total area; rank	110,567 sq. mi. (286,369 sq km); 7th
Land; rank	109,806 sq. mi. (284,398 sq km); 7th
Water; rank	761 sq. mi. (1,971 sq km); 34th
Inland water; **rank**	761 sq. mi. (1,971 sq km); 28th
Geographic center	Lander, 26 miles (42 km) southeast of Austin
Latitude and longitude	Nevada is located approximately between 35° and 42° N and 114° 02' and 120° W
Highest point	Boundary Peak, 13,140 feet (4,008 m)
Lowest point	Colorado River in Clark County, 479 feet (146 m)
Largest city	Las Vegas
Number of counties	17
Population; rank	1,206,152 (1990 census); 39th
Density	11 persons per sq. mi. (4 per sq km)
Population distribution	88% urban, 12% rural

Bristlecone pine

Las Vegas

Black Rock Valley

Ethnic distribution
(does not equal 100%)

White	84.26%
Hispanic	10.35%
African-American	6.55%
Other	4.38%
Asian and Pacific Islanders	3.17%
Native American	1.63%

Record high temperature 122°F (50°C) at Overton on June 23, 1954; and at Echo Bay and Laughlin on August 8, 1985

Record low temperature –50°F (–46°C) at San Jacinto on January 8, 1937

Average July temperature 73°F (23°C)

Average January temperature 30°F (–1°C)

Average annual precipitation 9 inches (23 cm)

Natural Areas and Historic Sites

National Parks

Death Valley National Park consists of 3.3 million acres (1.3 million ha) of the most complex geology in the United States. Due to its warm winter climate and its extremely hot summer climate, visitors can see unusual forms of animal and plant life, as well as interesting landforms.

Great Basin National Park offers outdoor lovers a chance to see many types of plants, wildlife, and topography. Especially popular is Lehman Caves National Monument.

National Recreation Area

Lake Mead National Recreation Area contains three of the Americas' desert ecosystems. Lake Mead's history ranges from its Black Canyon rock, more than 1 billion years old, to Fortification Hill, which is 6 million years old and a remnant of the last Ice Age.

National Forests

Humboldt-Toiyabe National Forest is divided into the Humboldt and Toiyabe regions. Humboldt has nine divisions, all within 2.5 million acres (1 million ha) of land. Its topographical features include alpine meadows and sagebrush lowlands, both of which make for outstanding hiking and exploring. The Toiyabe region also has varied types of landscapes because of its vast expanses. Especially popular are the park's Joshua trees in the Las Vegas district and the 12,374-foot (3,774-m) Dunderberg Peak.

State Parks

The state of Nevada oversees twelve state parks, four state historic parks, and six state recreation areas. *Lake Tahoe Nevada State Park* has a gorgeous view of Lake Tahoe and the Sierra Nevada from Cave Rock as well as fishing and boating. *Valley of Fire State Park* is named for its 200-million-year-old red sandstone rock, which looks like fire in the sunlight. *Cathedral Gorge State Park* is a rocky remnant of Pliocene Lake, which contained a 1,000-foot (305-m)-deep lake 3 million years ago. *Berlin-Ichthyosaur State Park* holds the turn-of-the-century mining town of Berlin and fossilized ichthyosaurs—fishlike dinosaur reptiles.

Sports Teams

NCAA Teams (Division 1)

University of Nevada–Las Vegas Running Rebels

University of Nevada Wolf Pack

Joshua tree

Mustangs

University of Nevada at Reno

Shakespeare festival

Cultural Institutions

Libraries

The Nevada State Library and Archives in Carson City contains materials on state government, history, and many other state affairs.

The University of Nevada–Las Vegas Libraries have information on academics and Nevada history.

The Nevada Historical Society Library provides genealogical resources as well as many books and articles on the state's history.

Museums

The Barrick Goldstrike Mine in Elko gives tours of one of the largest gold mines in North America.

The Southern Nevada Zoological–Botanical Park offers visitors a chance to see and learn about endangered animals and plants and their habitats. A popular attraction at the park is the Desert Eco-tours, which include a ghost town and the Old Spanish Trail.

The Nevada Museum of Art in Reno is the only accredited art museum in the state. Its permanent collection holds more than 1,500 pieces, ranging from art focusing on the Sierra Nevada and the Great Basin to contemporary artwork.

The National Automobile Museum in Reno has a permanent exhibit of 200 cars, as well as a variety of exhibits, a theater, and a visitor center.

Performing Arts

Nevada has one major opera company and one major dance company.

Universities and Colleges

In the mid-1990s, Nevada had six public and three private institutions of higher learning.

January–March

Cowboy Poetry Gathering in Elko (January)

Dr. Martin Luther King Jr. Birthday Celebration in Reno and Sparks (January)

Bristlecone Birkebeiner Cross Country Ski Race in Ely (February)

Snowfest at North Lake Tahoe (late February or March)

Annual Mother Earth Awakening Powwow in Carson City (March)

Desert Inn PGA International Golf Tournament in Las Vegas (March)

Rhyolite Resurrection Festival (March)

April–June

Easter Powwow in Battle Mountain (early April)

Harley Days in Laughlin (April)

Cinco de Mayo in Sparks (May)

Jim Butler Days in Tonopah (May)

Las Vegas Heldorado Days and Rodeo (May)

Carson Valley Days in Gardnerville (June)

Reno Rodeo (June)

July–September

Basque Festivals in Reno and Elko (July and August)

Nevada Rally International Motorcycle Race in Ely (August)

Nevada State Fair in Reno (August)

Shakespeare Festival at Sand Harbor, Lake Tahoe (August)

The Spirit of Wovoka Days Powwow in Yerington (August)

Great Reno Balloon Race (September)

National Air Races in Reno (September)

Virginia City International Camel Races (September)

October–December

Las Vegas International Golf Tournament (October)

Squaw Valley

Classic car celebration in Reno

To Find Out More

History

- Fradin, Dennis Brindell. *Nevada*. Chicago: Childrens Press, 1995.

- Siebert, Diane, and Wendell Minor (illustrator). *Sierra*. New York: HarperTrophy, 1996.

- Sirvaitis, Karen. *Nevada*. Minneapolis, Minn.: Lerner Publications, 1994.

- Thompson, Kathleen. *Nevada*. Austin, Tex.: Raintree/Steck Vaughn, 1996.

Fiction

- Kelso, Mary Jean. *Sierra Summer*. Springfield, Ore.: Market Press, 1992

- Kelso, Mary Jean. *A Virginia City Mystery*. Springfield, Ore.: Market Press, 1992

- Snyder, Zilpha Keatley. *The Runaways*. New York: Delacorte, 1999.

Biographies

- Morrow, Mary F., and Ken Bronikowski (illustrator). *Sarah Winnemucca, Paiute*. Austin, Tex.: Raintree/Steck-Vaughn, 1996.

- Ross, Gayle. *Dat-So-La-Lee, Artisan*. New York: Modern Curriculum Press, 1995.

- Sanford, William R. *John C. Frémont: Soldier and Pathfinder*. Springfield, N.J.: Enslow, 1996.

- Sanford, William R. *Kit Carson: Frontier Scout*. Springfield, N.J.: Enslow, 1996.

Websites

City of Las Vegas

http://www.ci.las-vegas.nv.us/

To find information about Nevada's largest city

Fleischmann Planetarium

http://www.scs.unr.edu/planet/index.html

To find information about the planetarium at the University of Nevada, Reno

Nevada Historical Society

http://www.clan.lib.nv.us/docs/MUSEUMS/HIST/his-soc.htm

To access information about the history of Nevada

State of Nevada

http://www.state.nv.us

To find information about the state government

Addresses

Nevada Commission on Tourism

Capitol Complex
Carson City, NV 89710

For information on recreation in Nevada

Nevada Division of Wildlife

P.O. Box 10678
1100 Valley Road
Reno, NV 89520

For information on fishing, hunting, bird-watching, or boating in the state

Wild West Museum

66 N. C Street
Virginia City, NV 89440

For information on exhibits and collections

Index

Page numbers in *italics* indicate illustrations.

Meet the Author

I'm R. Conrad Stein. I was born in and grew up in Chicago. At age eighteen, I joined the U.S. Marines and served for three years. After I was discharged, I attended the University of Illinois and received a degree in history. I later earned an advanced degree from the University of Guanajuato in Mexico.

I am a full-time writer and have published more than 100 books for young readers. I now live in Chicago with my wife (children's book author Deborah Kent) and our daughter, Janna.

Traveling is my favorite hobby. I have visited just about all the fifty states and many foreign countries. My trips to Nevada have always been exciting. In the Silver State, I avoid the glitter of Las Vegas. I prefer instead to explore ghost towns and lonely sites in the desert. Lake Tahoe and historic villages in the Virginia City region are also great places to visit.

When I am not traveling or working, I am consumed with reading. I find history books, historical novels, and biographies especially fascinating. Is there any subject more exciting than the history of the American West? I doubt it. Because I so love the spirit of the West, I was delighted to write this book on Nevada—a place rich in Western lore.

Photo Credits

Photographs ©:

AP/Wide World Photos: 46, 92, 121 bottom, 134

Carolyn Fox: back cover, 7 bottom, 8, 63, 76, 81, 95 top, 104, 116, 117, 124, 133 bottom

Corbis-Bettmann: 85 (Robert Holmes), 97 (Bob Simons), 42, 43, 44 top, 101 top (UPI), 73 top

Courtesy Secretary of State: 93

Dave G. Houser: 60 (Jan Butchofsky-Houser)

Envision: 112 (Peter Johansky)

Jay Aldrich: 7 top center, 7 top left, 16, 73 bottom, 98, 101 bottom, 106

Larry Angier: 7 top right, 12, 72, 94, 96, 99, 129 top

Liaison Agency, Inc.: 52 (Rick Carson), 49, 79 top (Hulton Getty), 107 (Rob Johns), 82 (Jim Selkin), 83 (G. Sioen/Rapho)

Nevada Commission of Tourism: 90 top, 122, 132 bottom

Nevada Historical Society: 13, 14, 19, 20, 22 top, 28, 29 bottom, 32, 33, 34, 35, 36, 41, 45, 47, 111, 119, 120, 121 top, 135

New England Stock Photo: 64, 131 bottom (Mark Newman), 62, 131 top (John Whyte)

North Wind Picture Archives: 22 bottom, 24, 25, 26, 31 bottom, 37

PhotoEdit: 11 (José Carrillo)

Ric Ergenbright: 2, 6 top left, 55, 109

Robert Holmes Photography: 66

Stock Montage, Inc.: 29 top, 30, 31 top, 40, 44 bottom

Superstock, Inc.: cover

Tom Till: 56

Tony Stone Images: 9 (Kim Blaxland), 58, 70, 130 (David Muench), 61 (R. G. K. Photography), 71 (James Randklev)

Unicorn Stock Photos: 6 bottom, 95 bottom (Dede Gilman), 79 bottom (H. Schmeiser)

Viesti Collection, Inc.: 6 top right, 54 (Richard Cummins), 6 top center, 15, 17, 38, 50, 53, 67, 68, 78, 84, 86, 89, 90 bottom, 113, 114, 128, 129 bottom, 132 top (Robert Mitchell)

Visuals Unlimited: 87, 123, 133 top (Mark E. Gibson)

Maps by XNR Productions, Inc.